Poems by Poets of the Roundtable

Eightieth Anniversary Anthology

Poets' Roundtable of Arkansas

Edited by Marck L. Beggs

Mockingbird Lane Press

Maynard, Arkansas

Poets' Roundtable of Arkansas

Copyright © 2013

All rights reserved. No part of this book may be used or reproduced by any means, graphic, electronic, or mechanical, including photocopying, recording, taping or by any information storage retrieval system without the written permission of the publisher except in the case of brief quotations embodied in critical articles and reviews.

Names, characters, places, and incidents either are the product of the author's memory or imagination. The publisher does not have any control over and does not assume any responsibility for author or third-party websites or their content.

Mockingbird Lane Press—Maynard, Arkansas
Library of Congress information in publishing data
ISBN: 978-1-62776-407-0
0 9 8 7 6 5 4 3 2 1

Library of Congress Control Number: 2013946703

Mockingbird Lane Press USA
www.mockinbirdlanepress.com
Cover Design by Jamie Johnson

Foreword

In the plainest terms, this is an anthology well worth reading—not just for the poetry itself, but for what the poems tell those who weren't there all the time and remind those who were of Arkansas life over the past eighty years. From the thirties to the present decade, from brick walls and sidewalks to barns and gravel roads, we rediscover ourselves. It's good that the poets are in alphabetical order by family name, for this puts the poems in no order at all by date, subject, or style, so that the reader—moving through the collection (I suggest) page-by-page—comes upon a new landscape at almost every turn.

Even so, the poems have much in common, and in the best ways. Nearly all of the language is conversational and is about the world of the reader. The poems are built of imagination, metaphor, compassion, wonder, and wisdom, with gratifying resolutions. Many of the poems are impressively written in established forms, while a good number are in *ad hoc* forms that serve the tone of the poem quite well. Sometimes I finished a poem with a true sadness; sometimes I laughed aloud. Often I smiled and nodded. More than a couple of times I asked my wife to pause in whatever she was doing so that I could read one to her.

Still, there's virtue in the fact that some readers will occasionally think, "This is not my kind of poetry," because every kind of poetry is included.

That's what a good anthology of this sort offers us. Most every remembered poet writing before us—from Shakespeare to Walt Whitman—may come to mind as one moves through the lines of these poems.

Many poems selected for this gathering clearly begin as the poet's and end as that reader's, who is likely to be saying repeatedly, "This must be about me!"

Welcome to some good hours with friends you may not have known you had.

~~Miller Williams

Editor's Introduction

I spent the summer of 2008 reading a few thousand poems by Arkansas poets, from the 1930s to the present. It was an exhausting, exhilarating, frustrating, and fulfilling task, to say the least. For the previous decade, I had published the *Arkansas Literary Forum*, an online journal featuring the best writers in the state in an effort to prove that Arkansas's literary insecurities were unfounded. After publishing new and original work by writers like Ellen Gilchrist, Miller Williams, David Jauss, Terry Wright, Jo McDougall, Kevin Brockmeier, Donald Harington, and so many others, I knew I had made my point.

However, there is much more to the story of Arkansas's literary tradition, and this anthology fills a rather huge gap, for these poems by members of the state's oldest and largest poetry society provide another thick portfolio of evidence to back my original assumption: Arkansas has some seriously good writers and we do not need to hide in the shadow of any other state in the Southern tradition.

Beyond all that, however, editing this anthology brought me back to poetry at its root: confronting the poetry of beginners to the poetry of some well-established, even sublime, poets.

According to Marcia Camp, author of the history of The Poets' Roundtable of Arkansas in the online *Encyclopedia of Arkansas:*

It all started in February, 1931, when a few ladies decided they wanted "to learn the fundamental, technical rules of regular, good, readable poetry." Mrs. Laura Lewellen invited them to her home, and they gathered around an old-fashioned round dining room table where Josie Cappleman, "a skilled craftsman in the poetic art," led the seven, which included Ruth Arnold LeVeck, Mae Loraine Bass, Stella Payne Crow, Marguerite Lanier Kaufman, and Bertha Meredith. The group grew to be Poets' Roundtable of Arkansas, the state's poetry society with branches across the state. Publication of the annual anthologies began in 1938.

Anyone perusing this anthology is about to read a lot of great poetry and, clearly, that is the point of any anthology. But first, I would like to draw your attention to the names of these poets.

Once a year or so, the *Arkansas Democrat-Gazette* features the odd names of various Arkansawyers, and I predict those editors will fall in love with this anthology, if not for the poetry (which would be a shame), but for the names alone.

Arminda, Lucille, Eloise, Annetta, Zelma, Ercil, Gladyse, LaNell, Geneva, Xuyen, Alma, Vera, Edsel, Daphne, Ernestine, Vada, Etta, Verna, Florence, Marguerite, Violette, Akers, Lily, Clovita, Dorrill, Dell, Valeria, Ninagene, Minnilu, Mamie, Lavon, Gretchen, and (my favorite) Rosa Zagnoni Marinoni—they just don't make names like that anymore. Or at least, we don't hear them enough. The fact that the spell-check on my computer just went ballistic suggests how great these names are. It is as if they were born to become poets.

This anthology represents Arkansas at its best, even for us academic types, for these poems do what poems should do: mess around with the reader's grey matter. It has been an honor to work on this project, and the rest is up to you, the reader.

~~Marck L. Beggs

Table of Contents

Arminda
    Guitar Man 1
Lucille Babcock
    Hawk and the Tree 2
Ted O. Badger
    The Predictable 3
Eloise Barksdale
    Four Haiku 4
A.G. Barnett
    Luck o' the Road 5
Annetta Talbot Beauchamp
    To Miss Effie—Bearing Spring 6
    From Wagon Wheels to Satellites 7
Zelma Bell
    My Marionette 8
Peggy Boggs
    Haiku Sequence 10
Mary Bolar
    Sharecropper Song 11
Iris O'Neal Bowen
    Death of a Star 12
    Count Again the Stars 13
Chester A. Bradley
    My Cherokee Great-Grandmother 14
Dora D. Brewer
    Satisfied 16
Ercil F. Brown
    Tater Wagon 17
    November Is An Analyst 18
    Robert Frost 19
Mary C. Brumley
    Rhymed Embarrassment 20
Gladyse Estes Bryan
    Pussy in an Old Hooked Rug 21
Jeane Burris
    Hobo Happiness 22
Roy Douglass Burrow
    Scarecrow Presence 23
Marcia Camp
    Nesting 24
    The Robe 25

Lily Carmichael
    To a Bereaved Friend 26
Jeanie Carter
    Dark Wonder 27
    Unstable Winds 28
    Troubled 29
David Barton Clapp
    A Busy World 30
    Sight and Insight 31
Virginia Wilkins Claxton
    River's Lament 32
LaNell Compton
    At Home 33
Martha Vickers Corn
    I Found A Cross in Flanders Field 34
    Silver Springs, Florida 35
Lillie B. Cranford
    The Wedding of Flowers 36
John Crawford
    Lines Written in Early Morn 38
Geneva I. Crook
    Restless Spirit 39
    The Old Mill 40
Stella Payne Crow
    Youth Speaks 41
    When Winter Calls 42
    Zingaro 43
Charles William Cunning
    Woodlawn Station—1944 44
    Gulf Deserted 45
    Lonoke County Rice Canal 46
Katharine Murdoch Davis
    The Gleam 47
Xuyen Van Doan
    Violence Is Not Included for the Heart 48
Alma K. Dougherty
    Pink Rosebuds 49
    Whispering Winds 50
Laura Mae Durham
    I Cannot Tell You Why 51
Liz Faulkner
    Gone Fishin' 52

W. Terry Field
 Elegy to the Dead in the Wilderness 54
Vera Blood Fletcher
 Contented Farmer 55
 You Spoke of June 56
Edsel Ford
 This You Must Know 57
 Remembered Thirst 58
Alice King Formby
 The Fawn 59
Daphne Virginia Fuller
 Moments that Bless 60
Jeanne F. Gallman
 Urban Renewal 61
Julia Matthews Gardner
 My Bluebird Inn 62
Violet Brugh Gingles
 Brotherhood 63
Adolph Oliver Goldsmith
 The Way Between 64
Ernestine Gravely
 Miss Lillian Emma Sue Mary Louise 65
May Gray
 When the Harvest Is In 66
 Sestina for the Santa Fe Trail 67
Sibyl Nichols Gutowski
 Night Train 69
Verna E. Hancock
 Voice in the Wilderness 70
Vada George Harkey
 The Ice Storm 71
 Autumn 72
Etta Caldwell Harris
 Some Dare 73
 Self-Impaled 74
 Pear-Tree Bouquet 75
Addie M. Hedrick
 Embers 76
 Night of Rain 77
Betty Heidelberger
 Vietnam 78
 Divorce 80
Kathy Helmer
 Where I'm From 81

Dean Henning
    The Escape 82
Ellis Doyle Herron
    Korea—1951 84
Delores Hinde
    The Happy Hour 85
Verna Lee Hinegardner
    Evening Meditation 86
    Visitor's Day at the Prairie County Orphanage, 1874 87
    Trapped in an Urn 88
Louise B. Hollowell
    Past the Valley of Shadow 90
Dodie Walton Horne
    Echo 91
    Outline for a Portrait 92
Bernice Humble
    In Memory Of 93
Stephen H. Humble
    Motherly Reaction 94
Florence Jai Humphreys
    And So the Harvest 95
Bess Ingram
    Ice-Box Blues 96
Neva Jay
    The Wind Is Aquarius 97
Martha Sherwood Johnson
    Shadow on the Snow 98
Patricia M. Johnson
    Lost Stones and Memory Fragments 99
Faye Williams Jones
    We Do Not Talk About It 100
Margaret Jones
    Blessing the Beans 101
Marguerite Lanier Kaufman
    Salute to the Pilgrims 103
Clara B. Keenan
    Chain Letter 104
Steve Ketzer
    They Do Not Take Heads at Sea 105
Rev. Howard Lee Kilby
    Pleiades Rising 106
    Nature Man 108

Anna Talley Kinnaird
    To My Flower Child _____ 110
    Prejudice _____ 111
Katherine Newman Krebs
    Dark Voyage: An Odyssey _____ 112
Patricia A. Laster
    Advent: The Coming of a Child _____ 113
    Blackbirds of Summer _____ 114
Ruth Brooks LeCroy
    Leaf Fires of Autumn _____ 115
Julie Cramer Lester
    And Truckers Don't Cry _____ 116
Nancy Jane Locke
    Poem for an Unspoken Love _____ 117
Rosa Zagnoni Marioni
    Marooned _____ 118
    Timberline _____ 119
    Humble Offering _____ 120
Patricia Washington McGraw
    Me and My Shadow _____ 121
Sister Mary Ricarda McGuire, RSM
    Innkeeper's Dilemma _____ 122
    Tomorrow's Tomorrow _____ 123
A.J. McIntosh
    My Broken Heart _____ 124
Catherine Moran
    Me and the Minotaur _____ 125
    Constructing the Building _____ 126
Robert Moore
    Loneliness _____ 127
    The Gunfighter _____ 129
Mary Hamilton Nery
    Ishtar Knew _____ 131
Olive Hering Nelson
    Her Man _____ 132
    Duck and Drake _____ 133
    A Sonnet to My Father's Hands _____ 134
Violette Newton
    Some Nights She Dreams _____ 135
Hien Duc Nguyen
    For Your Birthday _____ 136
Opal Jane O'Neal
    The Transition _____ 138

Marguerite B. Palmer
  Of Polyps and Men ... 139
  Hoard ... 140
  The Blind Song-Weaver ... 141
Akers Pence-Moore
  Toro Nagashi: August 6, 1984, Hiroshima ... 142
Gloria Okes Pekins
  Moon Rock on Display ... 144
Lily Peter
  For John Donne ... 145
  For the Flyleaf of Emily Dickinson's Poems ... 146
  Runes for Mathematics ... 147
Alice Waddell Portis
  Farmhouse Ghosts ... 149
  Hunter in the Valley ... 150
Gladys Powell
  Seacoast Honeymoon ... 151
  Language of Light ... 152
Jean Ravenscroft
  A Gentle Poet ... 153
Bonnie Reynolds
  In Defense of You ... 155
Clovita Rice
  Difference ... 156
Marnelle Haynes Robertson
  Earth-Hunger ... 157
  Matilda Jekyll ... 158
Barbara Robinette
  We Played Gin Rummy ... 159
Pearl Lunt Robinson
  Uncomforted ... 160
  Anonymous ... 161
Constance Rollins Rouse
  The Promise ... 162
Marie Morris Rushing
  Mental Celibacy ... 163
  Grandfather Knelt ... 164
  Furrow of Discontent ... 165
Ruth Wilson Scholl
  Frozen Landscape ... 166
Mary Bathus Schriver
  Winter Trees ... 167

Gladys Tillman Scott
    A Song to David ... 169
Dorrill Scroggin
    Psyche ... 170
Diana Sherwood
    Music ... 171
Richard Leon Spain
    Night Journey ... 172
Thomas Sperling
    November Dirge ... 173
Helene Stallcup
    The Power Switch ... 174
    Fish Eggs in Oil ... 175
Harding Stedler
    Equatorial Silence ... 176
    Nightmare Precluding Dreams ... 177
Kathryn S. Stone
    Fulfillment ... 178
Johnye E. Strickland
    Mother and Child ... 179
    Recurring Dream ... 180
Lew Taylor
    False Stones ... 181
Diane Taylor
    The Calling ... 182
Dell Teeter
    When April Knocks ... 183
Valeria Browne Thornton
    RFK ... 184
    To Peter I. Tchaikovsky ... 185
    Misplaced Woman ... 186
Ninagene Tillery
    All That Remained Were Reminders of Death ... 187
    Married Misfits ... 188
Anita E. Turner
    Enchantment ... 189
Patsy McKenzie Turner
    Common Factors ... 190
Neva McMillan Upton
    A Soldier's Love Letter ... 191
Peggy Caudle Vining
    Thanksgiving Time ... 192
    Prolific Dandelions ... 193

Ida Crane Walker
    Rx: Antidote For Loneliness in Children_____194
Jo Van Dalsem Wells
    Broken Lute_____195
Minnilu Whitington
    Day's End_____196
Elizabeth Wilkey
    On Hearing Wagner's *Tristan and Isolde*_____197
JoAnne Rennells Wilson
    Morning on the Lake_____198
Mamie Lou Wisener
    The Clock Has Ticked_____199
Anna Nash Yarbrough
    Face to the Sunrise_____200
Kitty Yeager
    Home for the Funeral_____201
Lavon Yepez
    Whirling Candy Stripes_____202
Gretchen Youmans
    This Gold_____203
About the Editor_____205

Arminda							1983

Guitar Man

Quiet evenings he plays
for me, his chocolate eyes
deeper than the wrinkles
on his face; and his fingers
know my melody.

Worn boots keep time
as fingers pick the strings
forearm taut with muscle's
blue tattoo twitching.
Shadows of whiskers, smoky grey
and soft, outline his mother's chin.
Once brown hair curls
over faded blue denim collar
neck bending, cheek resting
on his guitar to feel the music.

Fingers flow maple syrup smooth
though I know the feel of them
cracked dry,
and he knows
my melody.

Lucille Babcock   1977

Hawk and the Tree

She stood there
unabashed in her nakedness,
limb awry.
Her arms,
strength personified,
a haven
for his tired body.
She asked nothing of him;
she took nothing from him.
He slept
'til the sun
came out of hiding
and flared pink above the horizon.
Blinking, he
stretched his wings
and lifted himself with ease
into the wintry air currents,
leaving her
without a thanks or farewell.

Ted O. Badger							1996

The Predictable

Once as I was slicing a plum,
it suddenly occurred to me
that if your knife follows the line
indenting the side of the plum,
without fail, you strike the seed's edge.

We require the predictable
to give stability to life:
like such mundane things as washers
to halt the faucet's noisy drip,
or brake pedals to stop the car.

How often have I been upset
when touching the switch gave no light,
or the key failed to start the car?
If I'm expected to function,
I need predictability.

So it comes as a jolt to me
that friendship and love, of all things,
are the most unpredictable
experiences humans know.
The plum is far ahead of us.

Eloise Barksdale   1971

    Four Haiku

Arthritic fingers
  move cautiously through Bach Fugues—
    the Mockingbird's song.

Sparrows
quit fussing
the day of the eclipse.

Waves of ochre
  flooding rice fields—
    geese circling.

Pacific highway...
we drive slower and slower
under the redwoods.

A. G. Barnett   1951-52

Luck O' the Road

"I'll trust to luck 'o the road," he said
    When he left for Dublin town.
"I will not ride on the coach, bedad,
    At cost of a silver crown!"
"I'll sleep on a rick o' hay in a moor,
    I'll drink of a ripplin' stream,
I'll blarney a crust at a cottage door
    And likely a bowl o' cream."

But a maid came along in a creaking cart.
    "Patrick," she said, "hop in."
"An' how do ye know me name is Pat?"
    "By the tilt of yer nose an' yer chin."

"There's blue o' the sky in yer eyes, Kathleen,
    Wi' niver a trace o' guile."
"An' how do ye know me name's Kathleen?"
    "By the tilt o' yer lips when ye smile."

"Now why should ye traipse to Dublin town,
    Such a woeful way abroad,
Whilst me father is needin' a lad around
    To harvest the rye an' the sod?"

"Och! Then I'll joggle along wi' you
    Till we come to yer daddy's farms.
But work in the fields isn't all I'll do;
    I'll harvest yerself in me arms."

Annetta Talbot Beauchamp   2000

To Miss Effie—Bearing Spring

Spring moves up the river
a hundred miles a week.
It starts
small
and warm
and almost yellow.
From the Crescent City
the first sign comes;
a letter—
"My azalea budded out today!"
How many hundred miles?
How long before it's here?
I measure a map
in weeks—
but soon lose count.

Then early one March morning,
just a week of warmth away from me,
you found
three pussy-willow branches blooming.
You hurried north
through the bayous
and across the prairie;
you handed me a promise of spring—
wrapped
in damp paper.

Annetta Talbot Beauchamp   2001

From Wagon Wheels to Satellites

Time-borne creaks
of spokes
    and rims
       grind out their sound
revolving round and round
evolving
into satellites
    reflecting images
    deflecting words
echoes
    bouncing
       off a changing world
repeating and repeating
into nature's
    unchanging pattern of solstices
    and stars.

Zelma Bell   1939-40

My Marionette

I hold a puppet in my hand
It moves and speaks
At my command.

I made him (as best I could
From scraps of cotton
And of wood)
Just like myself, and there he is.

He looks well done
Of course I'm proud
And show him off to everyone!
He has the best I have to give
Everything, but breath to live.

If I could give him
Power of will
And let him move
From ribbons free
I wonder—oh, I wonder
What the end would be!

If I made others of his kind
To act with him upon the stage
And I should keep my station
In the pit above it all:
Turn them loose
And let them go.

Could I smile at what they did?
Or would I then be sorry
That my skill I thus displayed
As the greatest Puppet Maker
Once renounced
The dolls He's made?

Peggy Boggs   1984

    Haiku Sequence

Burying acorns
The squirrel creates chances
For a thousand oaks.

Digging in the snow
The squirrel barks at the joke
This first April day.

My iris bed is
Covered with tiny oak trees—
The squirrel scolds me.

Mary Bolar					1966

Sharecropper Song

I drag a cotton sack all day,
And pick a hundred, though I'm small.
There's no time to run and play,
So give me a doll to hang on the wall.

Soon the bales will be stacked high,
To bring some money to us all.
Papa, on Christmas, don't deny
Me a pretty doll to hang on the wall.

Mama, kill my guinea hen
To bake at Christmas; I'll go call
Her from the rafters in the gin,
But bring me a doll to hang on the wall.

A chiny doll with white kid feet,
She will look so proud and tall,
And won't be groomed; she'll be so neat
My little doll to hang on the wall.

Iris O'Neal Bowen   1965

Death of a Star

When I by chance behold a star in flight,
Free falling from its place in Heaven's plan,
I wonder if its journey through the night
Will end in glory, as it first began...
Or will the fire-washed comet, all aglow,
And showering light from countless years of space,
Unshackled from the sky that held it so,
Destroy itself with wild ecstatic grace...
Then, as it crashes through the atmosphere
And digs itself a black and molten tomb,
Will other stars look down and see that here
Lies sleeping one which gladly sought its doom?
    The star that shines the brightest and the best
    May long for darkness and a place to rest.

Iris O'Neal Bowen   1974

Count Again the Stars

When I was young and counted stars,
I could not comprehend
their quantity nor distance.
The night-blue sky sang couplets to my name
and each star asked an answer...Could I send,
far-reaching on their rays,
the thoughts I could not spell?
Yes, following their call, I found the start
of knowledge loaned to little ones.

I did not know my path, starting some eons ago,
when God's great finger wrote the words:
"Here at this place shall begin
a never-ending path."—I did not know
my path would lead only a little way
through verdant lands, along the troubled streams,
down highways built by busy men...

I did not know the shortness of this walking span,
but when men say "Infinity,"
I count again the stars, my stars,
and hear the sky sing couplets to my name...

Chester A. Bradley   1981

    My Cherokee Great-Grandmother
    (Talking 1885)

Our home was beautiful among the hills,
Cool springs gave forth their waters sweet and clear;
The rivers teemed with fish, and little rills
Danced in the sun where antelope and deer
Came down to drink and gambol in the glen
Among the willows and the cottonwood.
Then came the hosts of strange and greedy men
From far across the sea; our arrows could
Not match their guns; it seemed an open plot
That we be forced to move from place to place
Where food was short and hunger was our lot,
So now we had become a nomad race,
And then an order came from those in charge
That we be moved to distant lands, at last
Their soldiers came with guns, and by and large
We started out, so now the die was cast.

I was twelve summers when the march began;
We walked days past mountains, marshes and dunes;
Then crossed large streams on flimsy rafts and then
Went on through heat and cold for many moons.
At last we came to western Arkansas—
While they prepared a place some miles away,
But now their rules, the workings of their law,
Were cumbersome, and this prolonged our stay.
I now had grown into full womanhood;
Then came the young white men to homestead land
Nearby our camp, and then as fortune would,
I fell in love with one, he sought my hand.

The passing years have taught me to be meek—
As I sit on the cabin porch and smile
To see grandchildren play beside Jones Creek,
And feel a deep contentment all the while.
My heart has mellowed after many years,
I now forgive them for the trail of tears.

Dora D. Brewer   1938-39

    Satisfied

I ketches fish—
Ole 'oman fries 'em nice 'n brown.
I sits under 'simmon tree.
Sometimes goes to town.

Sun wakes me.
I goes to bed wid de chickens.
Sits an' whittles some—
Sometimes works lik de dickens.

Don't ask fo' much
Got a mule, a good 'oman fo' a wife;
Got some vittles, lil' ole cabin.
Mostly I sits an' enjoys life.

Ercil F. Brown   1954-55

Tater Wagon

I heard the tater wagon roll
across the frowning sky
and saw a whirl of martins tossed
like dead leaves on the fly;
The ripened grain, with heads bent down,
crouched in a pinched-up huddle
while wiggle-waggle waves went wild
on every pond and puddle!
The cows broke rhythm at the grass
and, lowing came to stable—
the wide brown eyes bulged out with fear,
their tails a shish of sable!

In childish fancy, like a dragon
wild and free, I drove the wagon—
cracked my whip at cringing earth,
and dumped out thunder in my mirth!

Ercil F. Brown　　　　　　　　　　　　　　1958-59

November Is an Analyst

November is an analyst;
　　She thumbs through summer's days
And finds her fruit, new-wealed,
　　On cellar shelves and weighs
The sagging load against the toll
　　Of winter's appetite,
She casts her calculating eye to barns
　　And bulging cribs crammed tight
With yellow ears—to mows stacked up
　　To pigeon-nested roof
With timothy and clover; then
　　To smokehouse where the proof
Of frugal hands is hung along
　　The rafters; sugared ham
And sausages in sacks that curl
　　Beside the quartered lamb;
To tables in the lean-to shed
　　Where pumpkins wait for pie
And strings or popcorn tied by shucks
　　And threaded peppers dry.
The woodpile has long rows ricked up
　　For cooking or for heat
Should winter come ahead of time
　　With snow and ice and sleet.
November is an analyst
　　And counts each stored-up thing
To see if we poor mortals have
　　Enough to last till spring!

Ercil F. Brown   1963

Robert Frost

Who now shall mend the broken wall—replace
The vagrant stones flung down by winter's rain,
Since you have gone to mend the walls where pain
Is known no more? And—who, though birches trace
The pattern of the snow? Who fill the space
Now void of song, along your wooded lane
When weary day creeps into bed—who gain
The pinnacle of praise with such a grace?

Along your way—the run, the wood, the wall,
You let the seed of simple living fall
To earth where miracles of sun and soil
Shall bring fruition to your lowly toil.
Would that my hands, Good Neighbor, could repair
Your fence—or this poor heart breathe song to air!

Mary C. Brumley 1940-41

    Rhymed Embarrassment

Had you heard
    That "Negro athletes excel whites?"
It's a word
    That humbles us self-esteemed "light."
Thoughts are stirred
    That question our heaven-willed rights,
Feelings blurred
    Might start something worse than mere frights,
Smiles demurred
    Could label us such petite sights!

Cheer the negro who earns his delight
Many times he has proved that he's bright.
Negro maids work long hours for a mite,
Garden men hoe from dawn until night;
When it's living on nothing but fight,
Playing blind to his black children's plight,
Daily singing his soul into flight;
Any negro excels any white.

Gladyse Estes Bryan   1964

Pussy in an Old Hooked Rug

Because she loved her cat and wished that she
Could save his likeness for posterity,
She dyed wool rags the shade of cherries ripe
In June. On this red background, strip by strip,
She worked the portrait of her pet in gray,
And she was gratified to have friends say
It was the image of old Tom...the cat
Lies stretched out on the rug, as sleek and fat
As he was in the flesh. She almost feels
He vanishes at times in quest of meals
Such as she used to give him long ago;
He looks continuously pleased, as though
Her hand still stroked his tiger-striped gray fur,
Each stroke rewarded by a throaty purr.

Jeane Burris   1971

    Hobo Happiness

I got no money in the bank
I got no title, got no rank
No fame and fortune follow me
But I'm as rich as I can be.

I got no house to call my own.
I got no car, no telephone;
I got no food here in my pack
My only home is a railroad track.

But I've more joy than I can hold
And laughter is better than gold,
While I am free to travel far—
No ties to bind, no cares to mar.

I got these clothes upon my back
And miles and miles of railroad track.
I got a lot that I could share—
I got a home that is everywhere!

Roy Douglass Burrow   1972

Scarecrow Presence

He
hovered
over my bed.

Fed
but not full
he came to me
through the fields.

He died
hungry,
poor,
and unfulfilled.

The corn is gone.

The scarecrow
remains.

Marcia Camp   1988

    Nesting

I heard a thud then saw a small
dun-colored wren reeling stunned
away from window pane that
wasn't there last Spring. Something in

her breast told her
an elm (that paid a grudging price for
progress) should be here. Again

she flew against my window,
betting hollow-boned frail body
she could find it.

"My nest now," I said, not in
arrogance but with regret—wishing
words could stop her headlong flight,
diminished now against the glass, as
she (persistent to the last) bounced off,
dimmed, leaving downy tufts of feathers
tipped with blood.

I felt a tiny knee or elbow move
beneath taut belly flesh to raise a
gingham wave across my dress,
knowing when my labor comes I'd
think of Mrs. Wren and
wish for her wild
mother-courage.

Marcia Camp   1989

The Robe

I lift it from familiar peg—your form,
broad hipped and shoulders bent, at last has worn
chenille's once softly tufted rows to clumps
like cotton stalks in winter, sparse and thin.
Young mother in another robe, transformed
into a surplice when sweet incense rose
in biscuit stream, you blessed with laden board
and waved a benediction from our door.
On care-worn evenings lit by kerosene,
your warm robe whispered bacon scent, while you
tied up the remnants of our day and planned,
as I do now, to pad a kittening place.
    A hearty tug could make it bird's-nest string—
    remembered love and robes keep mothering.

Lily Carmichael   1952-53

To a Bereaved Friend

This road is one you walk alone,
Although the way seems dark and far;
Your heart and soul are like cold stone,
Above you cannot see a star.

Yet in good time, through a long night,
You will awake and realize
The world moves on with the same might;
You will see things with clearer eyes.

You will take up the tasks again,
Though feebly at first it's true,
Yet each small task will lessen pain;
You will reach out for things to do.

Oh, there is peace and real true worth
With a flower garden to tend,
Just the feel of the good cool earth
Will help an aching heart to mend.

Find a small plot of ground to keep,
And when from pain you are so torn,
Hoe and rake and plant as you weep
Then sorrow will be easier borne.

Jeanie Carter   1978

Dark Wonder

I wonder
if the warmth of the sun
has color
or if the moon's coolness
has a special hue.
I wonder
if the boy my mother pays to walk
me safely to the bus each day
looks at me from eyes
dark like the darkness of my world,
or if he views
the girl who is me
through some sweet-colored iris.
I wonder
if he took my arm in a less
paid-to way
would the darkness lift
momentarily, and let me see
through the lens of love
the color of warm,
the hue of cool.

Jeanie Carter   1997

    Unstable Winds

The last time I saw Kathy
we sat on overhanging rocks
and watched a buzzard glide
on thermals, level with us
and the mountain top.

He came to us, seeming
to meet our eyes, looking
as if someone had shrunk
his head and put it on
with glue almost too dry.

Rocked by the wind, he showed
the underside of his wings,
pearl gray and as intricate
as lace on a bridal dress.

We swayed, mesmerized by his
easy, fearless approach,
seeing the wind lift and hold.

After she went over those rocks
two months later
and died seventy-five feet down,
I remembered that buzzard
and how the wind cradled him.

Jeanie Carter   2001

Troubled

The limit of my ambition is to lodge a few pebbles
where they will be hard to get rid of...
                          —Robert Frost

Many of your pebbles have lodged
in my heart and brain.

The road not taken plagued me—
I stood and wept
for what might have been
instead of relishing the road I took.

I couldn't agree on whether or not
fences made good neighbors
and often argued with you in the night.
Yes, I, too, am acquainted...

I've gone to the edge of those woods
where the thrush called you,
but I shut my ears to the call

and, like you, stayed out to watch the stars,
for the dark is always there
waiting to invite me in.

David Barton Clapp 1956-57

A Busy World

The farmer hoards his ripened grain,
The wild grapes trail the vine,
November geese are necking south,
The rivers float with virgin pine.

The steamboats round the river bend,
The cotton stalks are loaded white,
The orchard apples cheeked with red,
The summer day shows flood of light.

The blackbirds swoop the meadow clean—
The children seek a sunny slope
The sheep stampede a bit of green—
The hunters trail the antelope.

The spreading cloud gives down its rain,
The motor cars are tuned for speed,
The airplanes fly uncharted space—
On many hills the cattle feed.

David Barton Clapp   1961

Sight and Insight

If I could see the Spring returning,
With iris like tall candles burning,
If I could still my heart's deep yearning
To look upon my friends' dear faces
If I could glimpse familiar places,
My home, my garden, and their graces—
What glory that would be.

Yet thoughts like these hold not regrets
For fragrance show me violets
And listening to the cardinal sing
I catch the beauty of the Spring.
From absent friends I need not part
Because I see them with my heart—
How clear is sight to me.

Virginia Wilkins Claxton   1956-57

River's Lament

On the banks of the wild St. Francis,
Around old Madison town,
Camped the Osage and warring Shawnee
Where the river rushes down.
High on the cliffs above eddies
Stood the brave young Indian scout
To scan the turbulent river
And warn of the dangers about.

O, the warwhoop and chant of conflict,
And the songs by the warriors wrought
Are no longer heard on the hillsides—
The battles have long since been fought!
But if waves of the now quiet river
Could speak of the Indian's woe,
The legends would be of the heartbreaks
Endured in that long ago.

LaNell Compton   1945-46

At Home

I sit and look around me from my swing,
Everything is still the same today—
The swing is turned, and the shade trees cut away,
But that alone to me is no great thing.
Yet I have worn new eyes since I knew you,
That are no longer satiate with old sight
While groping for the glory of the Light
And for ethereal beauty, mystic, new.
For here drab Minnie Green is not unknown,
Dear wounded plans with happenings collide—
And even the morning glory vines outside
Have curled and browned and died where they
      have grown
And tossed blue bells this summer, O my dear,
Will they not bloom for me another year?

Martha Vickers Corn   1944-45

I Found a Cross in Flanders Field

I found a cross in Flanders Field,
Pale, gleaming in the snow,
And swiftly, with a breaking heart,
My tears began to flow.

Oh, shall I sleep in Flanders Field,
Where poppies sway and toss,
And shall my son pass that way too
And find my shining cross?

Martha Vickers Corn   1943-44

Silver Springs, Florida

The jungle flames in natural charm
Along that silvery stream,
Where bearded cypress trees reflect
Strange specters in its gleam.

The white boats drift with magic ease
On placid shimmering trails,
And like a dream, through crystal keels,
Wild beauty softly sails.

Long bridal grasses gently sway
In the heart of Sue-ille-ha;
And soft iridescent colors play
Rainbows on the Sagit-la-rah.

The lime grottoes and coral shell
Become exquisite tombs,
When light rays turn each prism point
Into Ethereal blooms.

Aloof Seminoles, the Mikasukees,
Camp by the glinting springs,
To dream their dreams of defiled gods,
And mighty fallen kings.

Lillie B. Cranford   1965

The Wedding of the Flowers

Once a rumor of a romance, whispered round
    among the flowers,
Made us think there'd be a wedding in this
    wonderland of ours.
Verbena told Petunia and Petunia then told me
That she became suspicious and hid behind a tree.
She saw the Morning Glories put some things inside
    the house
And she crept a little closer, being quiet as
    a mouse.
Bridal Wreath was on the table, and some Lady
    Slippers too.
And beside a pair of Fox Gloves, a Blue Bonnet,
    smart and new.
Pansy thought she knew the lovers, Columbine
    and Scotch Harebell;
Iris asked the Painted Daisies—but you know
    Daisies—they won't tell.
Black-eyed Susan was seen talking to Sweet William
    at the gate,
But she answered quite demurely, "It was just a
    casual date."
Calla Lily giggled shrilly when they thought it
    could be she;
Mignonette had caught her sitting on old Bachelor
    Button's knee.
Princess Feather blushed red-rosy when King Alfred
    kissed her hair,

But Camillia said, "That's nothing, just his
 continental flair."
At Four O'clock the church door opened;
 Jack-in-the-Pulpit took his stand;
Down the aisle came dainty Primrose holding
 Jonquil by the hand.
Dahila sang, "I Love You Truly"; Poppy gave
 the bride away;
Trumpet Flower played so sweetly, Tulip lost her
 heart that day.
Jimpson Weed was not invited. Did he worry?
 No, not he!
He was courting Calliopsis underneath a Willow
 Tree.
Thus, my dears, you have the story as a story
 always ends—
Nothing's caused so much confusion since the
 Wedding of the Winds.

John Crawford   1969

    Lines Written in Early Morn

Stillness pervades—a quiet
    that brings with it wonder,
    a beatitude that seldom
    comes in our fast pace,
    our meteoric race,
    life's paradoxical riot.
The quiet that cries out
    for soul searching
    contemplation,
    decision making: what is
    and what has been;
    what kind of creature
    this man who sits upon
    his throne of doubt.
Pouting, smaller made,
    lower than the angels,
    Adam moves—
    extends his hand.
    Casts his vote for
    better man,
    but somehow weakens, falters, fades—

Geneva I. Crook   1973

    Restless Spirit

Spirea, spotlighted against a backdrop of night
  Graceful white sprays undulating in a soft breeze,
    Created a waterfall of snow—
    A silent cascade of blossoms.

My spirit calmed—then, restless, begged a second sight:
  Wind from the approaching rainstorm shook the trees,
    Spirea fronds tossed wildly to and fro—
    A violent Niagra of blossoms.

Geneva I. Crook   1975

    The Old Mill
    (Lakewood, North Little Rock, Arkansas)

Men of vision build for the future,
    Build for posterity things that will last,
Whether by word, by painting or music,
    Or by creating structures in molds of the past.

Here's such a structure, conceived by a dreamer,
    In rustic setting at the foot of a hill:
The mill wheel of concrete with woodlike appearance
    Created by a genius with consummate skill—

Has steel bearings and axles to support and cut friction,
    Hand-riven shingles and rust-proof copper nails
Top the stone millhouse's wood sheaths and rafters,
    And a tree-like foot bridge has "limbs" for hand-rails.

The Old Mill in Lakewood is an Arkansas landmark
    Enjoyed by thousands these forty years past
And—thanks to men's vision—will enchant many others,
    For those sturdy dreamers built beauty to last.

Stella Payne Crow   1952-53

Youth Speaks

A strange big world invites us in,
As we give out with infant cry;
Then we are supposed to grin
For our proud parents—don't ask why.

Observing us they try to see
The color of our hair and eyes,
And which side of the family
Could claim us as a cherished prize.

Next memory's clock begins to tick
And count our problems as they grow;
That's when we need a measuring stick
To guide and check us to-and-fro.

Folks tell us how to live our life,
Take time for work, and time for play,
Extract the sweet, accept the strife,
And spread sunshine along our way.

Like Dad, like Mom, we want to keep
Our young hands firmly on the rope
Of Faith, be modern, too, think deep
Into ideas that promise hope.

From when we give our infant cry
To when we bid the world adieu,
We know our life may not comply
with all, no matter what we do.

Stella Payne Crow   1961

When Winter Calls

When winter calls on fields laid bare,
The merry snowbirds linger there
In search of seeds and scattered grains.
Upon the cold and barren plains
The sumacs bow as if in prayer.

Gaunt skeletons stalk everywhere,
And piercing winds now chill the air
With snowy flakes and sleety rains,
   When winter calls.

With frosted scarf around her hair
The brook assumes an icy stare,
And yet, while this white magic reigns,
The spirit of romance remains
To greet the spring, so debonair,
   When winter calls.

Stella Payne Crow					1963

Zingaro

While down a winding path I strayed,
A violin was softly played,
And listening to the music there,
I soon forgot I had a care,
Until I saw a vagabond
At rest beside a shady pond,
And as my noisy feet drew near,
He turned and gazed at me with fear.

"I'm just a traveler," said I,
"Strange friend, but could you tell me why
You chose this wandering way to live?
A settled home has more to give."

His voice was gentle as he said,
"I sleep with stars above my head.
I am a man of humble birth,
Who loves the simple ways of earth.
I cannot boast of any wealth,
But I am blest with glowing health.
Companioned by my violin,
I seek no other kith or kin,
I have no need of sympathy,
For God Himself takes care of me."

And I, the type who likes to fret
At trifles, now will not forget
All that is treasured is not gold
As this lone zingaro has told.

Charles William Cunning					1993

    Woodlawn Station—1944

My father was a listening man,
and while he ate, he listened—
not to my mother's hurried
words or to his children's
whispers, but for the crunch

of rubber tires on gravel
beds around our county
store, the slam of a wooden
door against its splintered
sash that called him back

to gasoline, ration books,
coffee beans, Lucky Strikes
and news from the Solomons,
the Philippines and France.
And watching from our back
store room, my mother

slowly stirred the soup,
hushed our taunts,
and listened.

Charles William Cunning   1995

Gulf Deserted

Pulling my coat around me, I stepped
back to oil-stained chat, broken
glass, cola caps and my father's
abandoned service station. Bypassed
years ago by the four-lane, now only
wasps, spiders and Dallis grass fight
over its two rusting pumps standing
at attention stuck on 29.9.

Closing my eyes, I hear an air
bell clanging, see my father
running; and smelling sweet
red-leaded gasoline, I remember hot
summers. The sound of tires
passing on the road behind
me awakens me to cold March
winds, and I see a hubcap rolling
slowly toward me, then circling
ringing as it settles
at my feet.

Charles William Cunning

Lonoke County Rice Canal

The pumps groaned as they pulled
deep, cold water up to Kitchell's
canal. I climbed the bank
and stepped through the willow
branches to look down into glass-
clear water. Bream and catfish
swam in slow circles ignoring
my fishing lines and clumsy
bait. It was July, but I felt
the cold penetrate.

In August I returned.
The pumps were silent;
the water warm and muddied.
A moccasin slithered quick
S's through the water.
That day I caught
poison ivy,
two small fish,
and the fever.

Katharine Murdoch Davis   1950-51

The Gleam

Like orphaned children in a moonless dark
The vast unthinking herds of human kind,
Wear out their days in ventures undefined
Attain no goal and leave no lasting mark.
Only their futile lusts relieve their stark
Low penury of spirit and of mind.
Crowded yet lonely, blind they lead the blind,
Flood-threatened yet too dull to build an ark.

And yet the scene is not entirely grim,
Though fiercely mortal's strive for roof and food.
Yet even amongst the lowest kindness thrives,
And rough hard men for others give their lives
With patient uncomplaining fortitude,
Which stirs to tears the watching seraphim.

Xuyen Van Doan   1977

   Violence Is Not Intended for the Heart

If violence is but a convenience
of people in haste
   (they don't have the time or the patience
   or the skill
   to untie the knots
   so they use scissors, instead)
Violence of the heart, then, is not a convenience
since it's sweeter than any other thing it faces
and still, such a victory—if any—is meaningless

If this era is the one of haste
and anyone who's slow
is dead
   (even ghosts are required to perform
   their apparition quickly)
the heart still cannot be in a hurry
since it burns every time it quickens its pace

If the mind claims itself the torchlight for Man
         to advance
the heart still has to grope its lonely way forward
since the mind, most of the time, is but a hitchhiker
in the heart's adventures

Alma K. Dougherty   1968

Pink Rosebuds

He stood in his olive-colored uniform
And she was close beside
She rarely ever left him
Since lately she had become his bride.
He reached up on a tall trellis—
Chose a pink rosebud with care,
And with a gallant gesture,
Tucked the flower
In her amber-colored hair.
Suddenly his blue eyes filled with tears—
She knew without a spoken word
He would soon be gone for years...
Or forever.

She stood on tiptoe and kissed him,
And he left her standing there,
Grieving—
With one pink rosebud caressing
Her lustrous, amber hair.

Alma K. Dougherty   1976

    Whispering Winds

In a drizzling cold rain he stood
on a crossing alone,
awaiting the slowing
of a grumbling freight train.
Each turn of the wheels
seemed a refrain, "Back to the road;
back to the road again."

If asked to analyze
what he was searching for,
how would he explain—
an open fire, a twinkling star,
and a grumbling freight train?
Or the fellowship of friends
sharing a pot of coffee or hot stew.
When his time was spent,
they would do what good pals do:
fold his coat over his bones
and sing old ballads in softened tones.
And when darkness fell, and all was still,
his requiem the wail of a whippoorwill.

Impossible to explain the allure of
spheral things:
wood smoke spiraling from open fires,
twinkling stars
and whispering winds.

Laura Mae Durham   1967

I Cannot Tell You Why

Green lace is on the trees again.
Should my eyes not tell me so,
My heart, attuned to nature's plan,
Would surely let me know.

This early-budding Dutch elm tree
Etched against the pale blue sky
Awakens longing deep inside of me;
I cannot tell you why.

Now, longing shall ever be my fate,
My love snuffed out at Spring,
Is there nothing, nothing to compensate
This surging, throbbing sting?

The soft spring wind that buds this tree
Leaves its caress upon my brow,
Stirs hope in the heart of me,
And I'll go on somehow.

Liz Faulkner   2006

      Gone Fishin'

We giggle,
three gals on a boat dock,
tangled poles, boxes of clumped worms,
chirping crickets, and no men
to bait our hooks.
We grimace, threading slippery worms
but smile when our corks nod.
Something flirts with our bait!

We squeal, clutching crickets,
their prickly bodies,
little hooks in our hands.
I cast my punctured bug,
lead weight sinking down,
flicking the rod
reeling in a little line,
working it like Poppa used to do.

A fish trails my bait!
Barbara yells! Her cork plunges!
I drop my pole
to grab garden gloves.
Jeannie takes our picture:
a sunny perch—maybe two inches.
We laugh at our "big catch."

No birds feed; turtles submerge,
making little ripples in the water.
Minnows appear to doze
in the water below the dock.

Not even foolish babies bite
in this mid-day heat.
Satisfied, we reel in our limp baits
and pass the handiwipes.

W. Terry Field   1963

    Elegy to the Dead in the Wilderness

Green were their gardens,
Smooth were their lawns,
Free were their pastures
From thickets and thorns.

Clean were their homes,
No dirt or decay;
Clean was their city,
They kept it that way.

There lie your forebears,
Parents, friends, kin;
Go gaze on the shambles
They're now resting in.

Go read on the tombs
Of those who rest there;
Then pray for a city
That seems not to care.

Vera Blood Fletcher   1946-47

Contented Farmer

Beyond the wood-plot, deep and dense,
You see him standing by a fence,
Surveying all his growing fields
In thanks for all the good earth yields.

For rugged strength in storm and stress!
While underneath a tenderness,
That only love of growing things
And deeper understanding brings.

When God and weather seem to band
Against him, while on every hand
New hazards threaten, through it all.
He keeps on working...spring and fall.

The joys that keep him satisfied,
Come from within...and will abide.
While poets sing of life in books,
He lives by noisy rushing brooks.

He learns the songs of native birds.
They sing the tune but leave the words
To him! Outsiders never know
His dreams...while ploughing row on row.

Vera Blood Fletcher   1950-51

You Spoke of June

All through the wintry months you spoke of June,
But now that June is here and earth abounds
With tender green, your heart is not in tune
With summer! Nor the gentle happy sounds
From feathered treetop tenants. Fluffed-out breasts
Still sing above the pool where goldfish play,
But now the mother-birds are garden pests,
No longer please. You look beyond...away
To far horizons. Mating calls at dawn
Still clock the day with musical alarms,
But you no longer heed them, stretch and yawn,
Or meet the day with eager restless arms.
What troubled yearning keeps your heart so sad,
The month of June no more can make you glad?

Edsel Ford   1947-48

This You Must Know

If I do not return, this you must know:
I had forgiveness in my heart at death.
I hold no grudge for those demanding, Go,
Defend your freedom with your dying breath;
But only pity when I realize
They knew no better way to keep us free
Than sending us to death with starry eyes
And hearts that sing, My country, 'tis for thee.

My heart is bitter, true, because I feel
My life is mine, and mine alone to spend;
But I forgive their foolish whims and seal
My faith in Him Who leads me to the End.
And may those pitied souls someday divine
This exile is their own instead of mine!

Edsel Ford   1947-48

    Remembered Thirst

He asked me if I wouldn't like to see
   Some other things; he had a new canteen
      The Army had released; and I said No,

Not now...recalling that eternity
   When I had trekked a chartless path between
      The jungles and the Nile's eternal flow.

How many times my thirst had to be slaked
   With honey from dripping desert stars!
      How many times I would have given all

I ever hoped to be, or would have staked
   My life's blood for a sip of wine! The wars
      Had left within my mouth a bitter gall...

Thanks anyway—they're good canteens, no doubt...
But not today—I think I'll look about...

Alice King Formby   1968

The Fawn

I lay close down beside the river,
My gun well-cocked, my heart aquiver.
The soft-tongued water murmured low,
Swinging the lily-pads to and fro.

The song of a bird fire-winged and throated
Upon the winds of summer floated,
While in nearby pools, alert and calm,
Great bass through lucent circles swam;

And farther on, a rushy brink,
A shadowy fawn stole down to drink.
I lay quite still, with half-closed eyes,
Wrapped in a dream of Paradise.

Then up I sprang with my gun drawn
With a keen desire to slay that fawn.
Where was it now, gone like my dream?
I heard only a fish hawk scream.

Daphne Virginia Fuller   1960

    Moments That Bless

I never disturb my little son
    caught lying on the grass,
Lazily watching a fleecy cloud,
    or bird that chanced to pass,
Studying the pattern of the leaves
    waving from the towering trees,
Or the flash of a colorful butterfly
    floating by on a summer breeze—
Or perhaps it is a grasshopper
    bending a lily pad.

Quietly left alone with his thoughts,
    he could be finding God.

Jeanne F. Gallman   1961

Urban Renewal

Down on the old street,
under the elms,
the houses are being torn down.

Back in the gardens,
where wrinkled hands have cared
for roses and spring hyacinth,
the earth is cluttered with boards.

Rare prisms of window glass,
wrenched from the beloved site,
stand idly under the trees;
and the porches are gone—
the porches and white painted rails
that held the laughter of happy years.

Under the eaves,
where the little dogs barked
at the paper boy riding his bike,
there remains nothing at all.

Where are the red sweaters,
the old sneakers and scrapbooks?
Where are the gliders and lilac
that hung the sun?

Down on the old street,
under the elm,
where the houses are being torn down?

Julia Matthews Gardner   1945-46

My Bluebird Inn

There is a spot I used to haunt
Early mornings on a jaunt.
It was on my father's farm in Spring,
And when the seasons brought the ring
Of the anvil, axe and hoe,
And of cowbells tinkling low,
Brought shrieking hawks and hooting owls
That preyed on birds and barnyard fowls,
It was then with skip and hop and jump
I took me to an old oak stump.

It was down a hill and through the corn,
Up to this stump where bluebirds born,
Maybe just the day before,
Were begging food—yes evermore.
Dad or Mother, with a worm,
Fed each baby in its turn.
Then when these had flown the nest,
Regretfully I ceased my quest.
I wish that I might once again
Go visit this, my bluebird inn.

Violet Brugh Gingles   1961

Brotherhood

The shepherd lad intently watched
The flaming star's flamboyant route,
But desert haze soon dimmed his view
And tribesmen heard throughout the hills
The music of his vibrant flute.
He did not know Omnipotence
Was changing molds of human lives;
That none, henceforth need walk in fear
Or cringe beneath a look of scorn,
For in the stable's hay-lined room
Man's love for man was being born.

Adolph Oliver Goldsmith   1938-39

The Way Between

From green to green is an endless way,
The breathing green at the pine tree's top
Is years away
From the sleeping green at its feet.

The way between from green to green
Is rough and hard and grating,
With never a place for the eye to rest
From the dull drab space between
The green.

Upward from the mossy green childhood
The way is irksome as pine tree bark,
With never a break in the roughness,
Never a twig to cling to.

Slowly climbing toward the living green
That is surely above,
Nothing can be done
Except perhaps to crawl
Under the shaggy bark to oblivion,
Hoping to irritate the life beneath
And cause it to thrust out a branch
Of green in protest
To break the brown bitterness.

Ernestine Gravely   1992

    Miss Lillian Emma Sue Mary Louise

She loved old Southern houses with hovering
tall trees like chapeau plumes atop their roof-heads
decorated with robin nests, leafy scraps of sky
and twittering swallows seeking twilight beds.
Concert of mocker's song, soft hum of bees,
wide lawns of waving grass and stately stalks
of larkspur, moving in late evening breeze
like Vivien Leigh's taffeta skirt when she walks.
Kind houses keeping wee paths that steal
through gardens, attic trunks, and pantry nook
for sugar cookies, stolen kisses, apples ripe to peel.
Firelight afternoons, snowy windows, armchair and
    a book.
  She lived in such a place.
To celebrate spring
   Miss Emma pressed the ribbon on her hat
   and preened before the pier glass;
Checked date and moon in Farmer's Almanac,
   potted a new geranium slip to trim her table,
   made sassafras tea and sipped it from a rosebud cup.
Then...winking at crocuses
   laughing in the snow outside her window
Miss Emma tossed her skirts and danced
   a little fling.
In style of Southern belle
to celebrate spring.

May Gray   1970

   When the Harvest Is In

A farmer knows untended boundary lines
And barren fields can cost a man his bread.
The wild creeps in with shrub and forest-pines
And only token crops are harvested.

I think the land will never quite belong
To anyone. The earth, serene and proud,
Sustains its own in silver tides of song
And wraps the sleeping in its emerald shroud.

May we, (attending the Edens we think we own)
Tend well the garden of the heart's domain
Lest, like Dives, we give as alms—a stone
Instead of bread; store high the golden grain,

And hear all night a weeping at the sill
Where Lazarus lies alone, abandoned still.

May Gray   1996

Sestina for the Santa Fe Trail

We reached the end of the Santa Fe Trail
before we reached this city of Holy Faith.
(The Conquistador's pious image is everywhere.)
The setting sun, like a blazing ball of fire,
paints the Sangre de Cristo mountain range
with its own name: the bright blood of Christ.

Against the skyline, like a saddened Christ,
the mountains rim the perilous muted trail
where once in grief, below the stricken range,
men suffered a pestilence that tried their faith—
and, helpless, saw it sweeping like a fire
upon the wind. Black Death was everywhere...

To the Pink Garter Saloon, from everywhere,
the sorrowing came, as if defying Christ.
They tried to drown the awful trial by fire
where Lamy marked the end of the trail.
But they could not forget the shape of faith,
and the gentle way of life along the range.

When we gaze from this majestic range,
we see the new, and the old, everywhere.
As if to reassert their father's faith
the bells peal out (in the name of Christ)
from every Mission on the sandstone trail—
their sundown windows like a bush of wild fire.

The "Land of the Little Bird" reflects the fire;
but the snow, unmelted on the mountain range,
cools the high sweet air along the trail
where Conestoga trains from everywhere,
and small cayuse once plodded past the Christ
of the Cross. This city of doubt and faith

is still the center of their hope and faith.
But even now—a thermonuclear fire
makes real our science-fiction tales. (Oh, Christ,
will the monstrous fireballs near the range
supply the needs of men everywhere,
or, hot as the sun's center, melt the trail?)

A peaceful trail, since still the ancient faith
is everywhere, bright as the tongues of fire;
strong as the range and peaceful as the Christ.

Sibyl Nichols Gutowski   1989

Night Train

A train whistle sliced through the starless night,
Its long, eerie sound hanging on the air
Above the murky marshes, a distant light,
Stirring me awake with its lonesome blare.
Like a living thing, despairing, it cried,
Ending shadowed movements, and not a stir
Was heard from places where night creatures hide;
Life was stunned into silence everywhere.

It fingered across furrowed fields of grain
And wide meadows of mist where wild life grows,
Still spreading its sorrowed and somber strain,
Bonding a feeling each living thing knows.
The lingering rhythm of wheel on rail
Was left in the wake of that mournful wail.

Verna E. Hancock   1951-52

> Voice in the Wilderness
> *The 1950 White House Conference
> on Children and Youth*

Dimensions of war menace
the height
the breadth
the depth of it
known not to the human mind
save only by the black-cast shadow
reaching back
before all knowledge,
running forward
beyond thought.

Even in that shadow,
there is a place
where thousands
stand as one,
demanding sunshine
for the children of the world.

Vada George Harkey   1973

The Ice Storm

Last night the rain fell softly
In the woodland,
But soon its drops were ice.
Cold wind brewed a storm
Leaving in its wake
Shattered, groaning
Trees, with white icicles
Hanging from their grotesque forms.
Creatures of the forest
Stared with astonishment
As day broke beyond the pond
Frozen over,
Where in the dusk wild geese found refuge.
The sun came up with warmth,
Forming cold prisms in the mist.
Drip, drip, soon the ice is gone.
Chaos reigns supreme.
Sacked of her beauty
The woodland stands trembling
With broken boughs.

Veda George Harkey   1974

Autumn

It's autumn in the land again,
The mocker trills a last refrain
Of time filled with extended bright,
And warmth and shade and pale moonlight.

The turning universe puts on
Her royal robes and meets the sun
At edge of day. The crickets sing
The harvest song, as wild geese wing
An arrow wedge above the wealds,
Above the ripened fields.

The horned worm spins his cocoon,
He knows the winter's coming soon.

Another night another day,
The sun in its accustomed way,
Severs vows in summer made,
When first the woodland violins played.

Too slow the hours drag at night,
The hoarfrost thickens like a blight,
And strips the leaves of gold and brown,
And drops them sighing to the ground.

Then winter comes to hold its sway,
And lovely autumn walks away.

Etta Caldwell Harris   1958-59

Some Dare

Now they who walk within this boundless night—
So near the jagged rim, unprobed and deep,
May snatch some lighter moments of delight
Before they close their eyes in final sleep.

If briefly that enchanted foreign sun,
With splendor from a bright day-world apart,
Should, glowing on although light-span is done,
Leave satisfying stillness in the heart—

It is because some dared to grasp a reed,
With heart and hand, and climb it like a vine,
Until they wrung life-blood from every need,
To sparkle in their cups like purple wine.

Let those who falter on the wall of night
Learn, unperturbed, to look on far-flung space,
Undaunted, grasp brief moments of delight,
And drain the sweets from this brief resting place.

Etta Caldwell Harris   1962

Self-Impaled

I hang on living wood,
To which I am impaled by my own thoughts,
From which no one can bring me down.

Through days unseen
And nights undreamt
I listen, unavailing.

I search, I wait, I hope—
Blind-eyed, unblinking,
Uninvited.

Patience is my name,
Who seek the fire
To set my uncommitted realm alight,

By no more right
Than had the sun
To set a private course.

Yet I still cling
To living wood—
No one can bring me down.

Etta Caldwell Harris   1970

Pear-Tree Bouquet

Here, leaning to the south wind,
Lone tree, blooming fully,
Gathers itself into a great bouquet
That sheds its fragrance over the acreage,
Beautifying an ancient site
And furnishing a loft for choirs of birds.

Except for the hardy pear tree,
The century-old orchard is gone,
Leaving views through open spaces
Where the aroma of peaches and apples
Once blended with pears and plums
To concoct wine for spring-dizzy bees,
And later to furnish morsels
For any boy lying in the shade.

Only one twisted tree still blooming,
But, oh, what beauty, what fragrance
And what memories
Are pink-ribboned into this bouquet
Bride-thrown from other days.

Addie M. Hedrick   1945-46

Embers

The hour grows late and only embers linger
Where leaping flames once filled the room with light;
Slowly these flicker out, a graying finger
Of ashes creeps across the hearth, and night
Steals quietly in to work its chill desire.
And I must rise to go reluctantly.
Musing, the while I watch the dying fire,
How very like to life a fire can be,

For all things burning turn at last to embers;
Youth is a flame soon spent and we are old,
Love but a story that the heart remembers
Warming itself before a hearth grown cold.
Forgotten hopes, lost dreams, peace after strife—
Embers of youth, embers of love, of life.

Addie M. Hedrick   1954-55

Night of Rain

All night we listened to the wind's longbows
Twanging as piercing arrows of rain
Battered the dusty armor of the fields
In furious assault. The captive grain
Strained at its loosening bonds; rebellious corn
Lifted long lances eagerly, and grass
Stood blade to blade, waiting; reluctant weeds
Crouched in the fence rows...Hearing the thunder pass,
Urging the archers on to other hills,
We rose and went outside to find the shaken
Forces of drouth in riotous retreat,
The rebels drinking deep, and the farmstead taken.

Betty Heidelberger   1975

      Vietnam

If
  it's
    supposed
      to be over,
Why
  can't
    I forget
      the soul abuse
        and nothingness.
We
  read
    the paper
      and say,
        thank God
          it's over
While
  widows
    cry
      in
        empty
          beds,
And
  children
    live
      in
        glass
          houses:

```
You
   say
      it's
         over,

I
   say
      it's
         just
            begun.
```

Betty Heidelberger   2001

    Divorce

I go mellow into the morning
stretching cat-like toward
familiar contours and warmth
finding only memory,
a note that says you're gone,
some clothes left behind.
The afternoon hangs on strings
and I, a giant marionette and you
the puppeteer, still mold me
into your mood.
Dream-like
I stumble into evening,
drink, play your favorite music,
a sleep walker
running from the night.

Kathy Helmer   2007

Where I'm From

I am from sugar cane field,
Evangeline Maid bread dipped in cane syrup.
I am from a house on cinderblocks,
a front porch with a rocking chair and swing,
and the fragrance of chicory-laced coffee.

> I am from fig and pecan tree, azaleas, and rice.
> I am a blend of a Cajun mother and
> New York Yankee father,
> from Dorothy Begnaud and Charlie Hahn.
> I am from the hard-working immigrants
> from France and England, Wales and Germany.
> From "pulling your share of the load"
> and "eating everything on your plate."
> I am from attending Sunday School
> and singing in the church choir
> at the little white Methodist church
> in Alexander, New York.
> I'm from Breaux Bridge, crawfish étouffée,
> chicken gumbo, andouille and boudin sausage.
> From the German POW camps of WWII,
> escaping religious persecution,
> and the pursuit of freedom and happiness.
> I am from a backyard swing set,
> rosaries, poodle skirts, and bobby socks,
> Elvis, American Bandstand,
> the twist, and Rock and Roll.

I am all that's good about America.

Dean Henning   1994

    The Escape
    (according to legend)

In old Norway, in the city of Oslo
lived a man named Ahlee.
Rather reluctant to work,
one day he donned a wig and a dress,
fetched a sack and strolled to the bank.
On the steps he lay till sunset.

The door was no match for Ahlee's expertise.
With candle in hand,
he crept inside and paused at the safe.
Before the candle burned out,
he stuffed all the money into his bag.
He paused on the front steps for a nap.

Not long after the sun had risen,
he was awakened by the barrel of a guard's rifle.
"What have you in the bag m'am?" asked the guard.
"Why it's only rags," replied Ahlee.
"Ah let me have a look," replied the guard.
"Really it is all the money in the bank," replied Ahlee.

"Be on your way m'am," shouted the guard.
The next day Ahlee met
a needy friend and lent a generous helping hand.
The curious constable arrested Ahlee
and placed him in the fortress.

Ahlee dug a freedom-tunnel with his hands.
But when he was seen about town,
he was arrested and placed in the fortress.
He threw a length of rope over the wall.
Again he was seen about town,
arrested and placed in the fortress.

They placed five guards over Ahlee.
After sunset,
Ahlee secured his belt about his neck
and tied the other end on a bar.
he then stood on a chair
for his final escape.

Ellis Doyle Herron   1965

    Korea—1951

Our brother is dead.
He was your brother,
he was my brother.
Must this plucked flower
of sweet youth,
be decorated
and forgotten,
while the heated crucible
distills blood and gold
into this ramification
called humanity?
As decorated drones,
personifying man,
seated around
the parlay table,
some saying, "no,"
some saying, "yes,"
while cold gaping mouths
yawn in grim reality
on forgotten fields of honor, drink water
from gentle rains
sent to replenish
the earth.
Here lies our brother,
with only a bleak,
broken slap bearing witness,
in eulogy,
to a veneered civilization
that piously cries,   "Amen!..." "Amen!..." "Amen

Delores Hinde   2005

>   The Happy Hour
>   A parody on "The Children's Hour"
>   by Longfellow

Between the midday sunset
When muscles are losing their power
We end the day's frantic bustling
To meet neighbors for happy hour

Down the lane we hear voices calling
Above shuffling of our friends' deck chairs
As timely discussions are solving
The world's many problems and cares

A handshake or backslap in greeting
Makes all folks relax at ease
Tinkling cool glasses are toasting
Thoughts riding the soft summer breeze

Tomorrow we'll gather at Charlie's
Or at Doug's our glasses may clink
Grateful these welcoming neighbors
Build friendship's strong golden link

Verna Lee Hinegardner   1968

Evening Meditation

Alone, confronted by myself, I hide
From me, ashamed to face my day at night.
When I arose this morning twirling time
Encompassed me. A swelling tossing tide
Of duties lashed back in hateful ways. The grime
Of petty thinking stained. Now I must climb
Confining barriers to see the light
Surrounding me. "Lord, help me understand
Myself. Again today I lost the fight
To consecrate my life." God did not chide.
I felt Him touch my calloused trembling hand
And it was still. I heard His crisp command,
"Sleep well, and face the morrow purified."

Verna Lee Hinegardner   1985

Visitor's Day at the Prairie County Orphanage, 1874

Lined up with all the others, Sunday clean
shampooed and showered, hair pulled tangle-free
behind her ears in red braids clamped with green
barrettes, shrewd-eyed and freckle-faced Marie,
in ruffled nearly-new green dotted swiss,
stands quietly. Arms hanging down, feet spread
apart enough to wait, she knows she'll miss
hands touching hands like beads of knotted thread.

Two hours are ten hours long just standing there
while would-be parents stare and quickly leave
to interview the lucky kids who, square-
shouldered, file past to move away—or grieve.
Her pleading eyes that burn a red hot brand
say, "Need a little girl with no right hand?"

Verna Lee Hinegardner   1988

Trapped In an Urn

Bottled in this rose decorated
teal blue urn, I yearn to escape.

Whoever thought of trapping my
cremated ashes and burying
me, urn and all, on top of Myra
must have been insane.

Sure, she was my wife, but there
was life, lots of life, after Myra.
Myra was no untainted saint,
and I could have told her mother
a thing or two—but bronze
it had to be, even though the cost
was up to me.

Myra had more headaches than any
man could stand, and then one day
I came home too early and learned
the reason why. From that day on,
I stayed out late, sometimes all
night. Then finally we went our
separate ways
until she came out here, by hearse.

And now I'm cursed, sitting like
a sentry above corroding bronze;
and even Myra wouldn't want me here.

Perhaps one sweet day, the earth
will shake and take away that glob
of sod above me and crack this urn
so I can return to dust.

Louise B. Hollowell   1962

    Past the Valley of Shadow

My soul shall go to rest in quietude
And peace, sleeping alone in the deep
Of a long night, fearing no darkness.
The wonder that is Spirit
Shall leap past unwasted stars
To the glow-of-gold and jasper halls,
Where desire is fulfilled and sorrow forgotten;
Where joy is beyond all telling.

Dodie Walton Horne   1962

Echo

On a slate sky
Are scattering flights of compassless birds:
Plaintive punctuation
To a bleak November day.
Walking in sturdy boots,
I shiver, look up, and hear
Fragile, uncertain sound.

Though ground and sky
Be divided by horizons;
Though birds may find
A respite from the snow;
I listen, and silently echo,
For I know,
      I know
How hard it is to know which way to go.

Dodie Walton Horne   1976

    Outline for a Portrait

Early on, the story man
Seeks
And finds a way to share;
Chooses
To be magnet, draws
The myth and magic hovering;
Echoes
Fierce battles, misty dreams
That listeners recognize and know;
Re-kindles hope of more than these;
Weaves legends into tapestries...
His portrait should show
Horizons in the background,
Stories in his eyes.

Eyes that listened thus
Retain
Montana sky, Virginia rain;
Reflect
Endurance greened from tracking
Inner wilderness,
From moving sometimes with the wind;
Remember
Keenly in his time's
Kaleidoscope of scenes:
A glow of chosen faces,
Shoreline solitude,
The bricks in Richmond,
Telling lines in hands.

Bernice Humble   1976

In Memory Of

In memory of a boy that called me Mom,
Who volunteered for war in Vietnam;
Where is his bright smile of childish delight,
While marching with buddies "left-right, left-right?"

Fortunate ones returned to friends and wives.
Others, like ours, paid full price with their lives.
Condolence from a great government head
Would never fulfill one waiting to wed.

Mounted on velvet his medals are framed,
A meager reward for a young boy maimed.
With sweet memories and a broken heart—
In deep concern we are never apart.

Government citations, a folded flag,
A necklace bearing a numbered dog tag—
All hang beneath a familiar snapshot,
While his body lies in a soldier's plot.

His bronze star we accept with all due pride
And wear a small gold star because he died;
But these regal honors can hardly suffice
For his life—a stark undue sacrifice.

Stephen H. Humble   1978

    Motherly Reaction

A golden moon begins to dim its light,
As leaves surrender to a shifting breeze
A pausing fawn cautiously brings delight,
And soon prepares to drink in gentle ease.
A cloud intends to bank the frightful sky,
As lightning flashes by the wooded lake.
Asleep inside a patch of reed nearby,
The mother doe, disturbed, is quick to wake,
As angry clouds release tremendous might,
A burning pine is falling to the earth.
The mother's quick response returns in flight,
To save the fawn that she had given birth.
        A frightening moment takes her by surprise,
        But daring moves put joy in mother eyes.

Florence Jai Humphreys   1956-57

And So the Harvest

Man has furrowed the sky and sea
From Hiroshima to Bikini,
And sown strange seed which he has wrought.
What he shall reap is food for thought!

Up from the fury of war, the stench
Of fear and death, horrors that wrench
The soul and defy the spirit's release,
Spirals man's hope for wars to cease.

How futile, man's strife for peace!
Grace, sufficient for all release,
Love without merit, sets men free.
And so...the harvest that is to be.

Bess Ingram   1948-49

Ice-Box Blues

An electric refrigerator is really fine;
For my ice-box, tho, at times I pine.

The new one works according to plan—
But how I miss that young ice man!

It was part of the routine of the day
To see the iceman come this way.

I hope no other household joy
Will sacrifice the grocery boy.

The new ice-box saves lots of time
And to frown on it would be a crime,

But I miss the iceman very much—
He sorta gave ice a human touch.

Neva Jay   1973

The Wind Is Aquarius

The wind is colder than a witch's heart
It's wilder than a gypsy serenade
It whispers through the pines and often starts
To flirt incessantly along the promenade;
It dances like a dervish whirling dust,
Then waltzes as a maiden 'round a hall;
In summer kisses roses—as it must
Capricious as a gallant at a ball.
It flies a child's first kite, sometime in spring,
Or takes to wings as aircraft pierces blue.
It can't be tied by knot of unseen strings,
And yet, it's there—a gift for me and you.
Unowned by man, the wind is fancy free
To challenge stars, or yet, embrace the sea.

Martha Sherwood Johnson   1949-50

   Shadow on the Snow

Here at the end of devious rabbit run
Carved on a winter meadow
Its agitated, frightened shape
At end of shallow burrow.
Inherent with the fear that clings
To all small frantic poor wild things
Who may not see tomorrow
Because, and all too soon, they know
Through man or dog or grinning gun
Another of their timid kin
Will turn etching, scarlet-done
Against the sorrowing snow.

Patricia M. Johnson   1991

   Lost Stones and Memory Fragments

Today when I explore this southern trail
And stumble on a long forgotten stone,
I feel my color drain to deathlike pale—
Somehow a presence—I am not alone.
Could we have walked among the cypress greens,
Along this bayou in another time?
Do I imagine skirts of crinolines;
Are we a part of past life in pantomime?
I touch the broken slab among the leaves,
But moss has covered any trace of name.
The undergrowth of feeling—I'm aflame
   With memories I cannot seem to trace;
   Oh, why am I attracted to this place?

I look beyond the dense of thicket wall
To see white columns standing in the mist.
I sense my shoulders wrapped in sequined shawl
Near this plantation. How does it exist?
The doorway opens wide; you take my hand
And draw me to a dazzling banquet room
Where servants briskly move at your command;
I am bride and you, My Love, the groom.
The music starts and we must lead the dance
In ballroom staged below a curving stair:
Two figures in a dream of old romance—
We waltz, and then you vanish in the air.
   You find me on the trail, face streaked with tears;
   The time is now. Where are those hundred years?

Faye Williams Jones   2007

We Do Not Talk About It

A shadow slinks around the cars—
not seen, but not unseen—
in the parking deck.

Going to work in rush hour,
we talk on phones, clutch briefcases,
nod to acquaintances.

We walk by art galleries' vivid colors,
restaurants' garlic and grease aroma,
sounds of jazz blends with traffic's discordance.

In urban renewal on the city's riverbank,
we do not let imagination roam
and ignore the aggressive homeless.

In the blinding sun we pretend
a bobcat does not bask in the sun
on the brick wall.

Some things we don't talk about.

Margaret Jones   2000

Blessing the Beans

The warm aroma of speckled pinto beans
simmering in salted water
brings back the Klamath River in 1965,
Jerry and me working in tiny school
near Hoopah Indian Reservation,
old Miss Hannah serving pinto beans
in bowls and rolls every Tuesday.

First day of school, during lunch,
children file in, sit at long table,
Miss Hannah ceremoniously
asks Jerry to say grace,
thick braided heads bow
in practiced obeisance to White Man's God.

While the children waited,
Jerry glanced over
like a wild-eyed deer
stalked by a grizzly.
Ever slick with words
he made it to amen
with no one the wiser.

Many a sloe-eyed child would eat nothing
between noon and noon though father
would have his bottle and his smokes.
They even came to school when feverish,
bundled up by greasy-haired mothers.

Still smelling pinto beans,
I wonder if Jerry ever says grace
when they bring his pinto beans to him
down in solitary.

Marguerite Lanier Kaufman   1986

Salute to the Pilgrims

*But at length they found water & refreshed them
selves, being ye first New-England water they
drunke of, and was nowin thir great thirste as
pleasante unto them as wine had been in for-
times.* --William Bradford, *Plimoth Plantation*

You have drunk the new water, and now you are tied
With bonds more enduring than gold or than pride;
The land is now yours—you belong to the earth,
That you touched with your hands,
When you drank to new birth.

For those who came early—let us who live now,
Recalling our heritage, make a new vow;
We drink to the covenant that sets us apart,
With a song on our lips,
And a pioneer heart.

Clara B. Keenan   1948-49

Chain Letter

Her letter stated, "If you copy this
Five times, mail each, unsigned, to some young friend,
Great blessings will fall on you; if you send
It not, calamity and nemesis..."

So straightway, wishing not to be remiss,
She soon had five clean copies penned
And posted—then awaited dividend
In blessing, doubting not the promised bliss.

And so great blessings came upon her life,
The first one being this experience;
But soon, too, came calamity and strife
And plied her with an equal diligence.

I had, but copied not, a like chain letter—
My bliss nor my distress, nor worse nor better!

Steve Ketzer   1982

They Do Not Take Heads at Sea

Being raised by the Pacific,
having felt the sand like quicksilver
running beneath my feet in the fringe,
and having fled the breakers
instead of riding them out—
I would change.

Having seen the sailors
with their pandas in San Diego,
and having weighed the pay of dissolution
against this landbound existence
that seethes like desert sand and rain—
I would change.

Having talked with fishermen,
and having walked their hard bound boats
that creak and groan for deeper seas
while pelicans pout on the mast,
and having asked what their nets yield
on this side and that, learning
they do not know all the net yields—
I would change.

Being raised by the Pacific,
having searched for shells with my feet
until my back blistered in the sun,
conscious then and knowing now
that anything at all is one—
I would change, I would change.

Rev. Howard Lee Kilby   1981

Pleiades Rising

Tonight I sit alone, so emptily,
an old Zen poet listening to his breath
watching midnight stars rising
    above November trees
and her Maxfield Parrish eyes
    in my memory.
The first time I saw her—I stopped.
Don't ask me why, I can't explain.
Total strangers on a cold afternoon
standing among Cadillacs in a January rain.

The second time, by accident, we met again,
It was the same as before.
My heart lay pulsing on the floor.
She and I, two tourists on a mountaintop
during an August thunder and lightning
storm in North Carolina.

And then one day, in Hong Kong, her lips
touched mine...White clouds, her perfume,
butterflies filled the universe, and the
Chinese Conservatory Orchestra played
around us, marching through the room.
Firecrackers exploded...Kung Fu warriors
lifted the cosmic dragon in his dance
to the beating drum, the beating drum.

Tonight I sit alone, so emptily,
an old Zen poet listening to his breath
watching midnight stars rising
above November trees
and her Maxfield Parrish eyes forever
   in my memory.

Rev. Howard Lee Kilby   1995

Nature Man

His blue eyes told the story
with a certain nobility of mind
as when all things were pure,
gentle, innocent and kind:

"One spring day, a gray squirrel
was in the backyard.
I tossed him a slice of bread;
he grabbed it and ran up a tree,
stopped and looked at me.
The next day, he was back again.
I tossed some bread to him,
he took the bread and ran.
That summer, he came closer and closer
until finally, he would take the bread
out of my hand."
Daddy smiled a smile
Mother Teresa would understand.
"When the trees were bare
I saw him there, at the kitchen window.
I held up a piece of bread
and he pawed the glass trying to get in.
I raised the window, handed him the bread;
he took it and scampered off.
After that, whenever he wanted something
to eat, he'd come and tap on the window."
He finished his story and smiled.

I guess it will be my job now
to learn how
to feed wild squirrels
at the kitchen window.

Ann Talley Kinnaird   1998

To My Flower Child

It was always Woodstock,
making itself known, like a snake
curled inside your shirt. You didn't
have to be there in the mud; it was something
in the air you and your buddies
breathed in sixty-seven,
making you risk a little more, yearn
a little more, ache a little more
for something out there just
beyond your grasp.

Dreamer, said your fourth grade teacher,
and you said, Yes, to her; I was in
my head on a pinto pony while you
did nouns and verbs.

> You stood and watched
> your daddy work with wood
> and wondered if you had a talent
> other than guitar,
> or if you'd ever land
> a Wildcat on a carrier as he had.
> The not-knowing look took its toll...

Today you feign establishment,
but we know, you and I, of the beguiler
coiled against your heart:
and we know that still, a pinto pony
brings that diamond back into the light.

Anne Talley Kinnaird   2006

Prejudice

My feeders and my bath
are for the good birds with bright
color and refinement:
cardinals
blue jays
wrens and finches.

But multitudes
of rude panhandlers
sparrows
pigeons
blackbirds
swarm the seed and splash
the water like grubby children
in a public pool, crowding out the *rightful*.

It is the *beautiful*
and *civilized* I want in my backyard:
the scarlets
yellows
bluebloods.
so I hammer
on my window, to scare
away intruders, and make
room for those I choose to board.

Had I the nerve,
I'd get a gun and shoot the bloody horde.

Katherine Newman Krebs   1990

    Dark Voyage: An Odyssey

My trembling fingers
touched the alabaster walls
encircling the Mosque of Mohammed,
as I pondered the mysteries of Egypt's land.
What secret does the human-headed sphinx
still guard at the three pyramids of Giza?
What dark enigma shrouds the Pyramid of Khafra?
I listened to the echoes
of the Nile—the mystic beat—
and sensed a strange exhilaration
such as Cleopatra must have felt;
hypnotic trance, welcoming the unknown;
the faster pulse before the asp
released its venom.
And the Tomb of Tut-ankh-amen:
what treasures wait within the sepulcher
of this golden boy-king there in Luxor?
Surely a curse would strike
the strongest-hearted fool
who dared to look upon his mask,
to touch a gem
or violate the paintings on his tomb.
Oh, ancient land of Pharaohs and the Nile,
I traveled far to probe your mystery and intrigue,
but left with only fascination for your past.
I wish I could have seen you with my eyes.
But I must journey via Braille,
on fingertips.

Patricia A. Laster   1993

Advent: The Coming of a Child

I.
This Advent will be more serene
Since I'm no longer organist—
No preludes, hymns or antiphons—
And time I spent in pressured haste
Is now revered as private space.
No preludes, hymns or antiphons
Since I'm no longer organist.
This Advent will be more serene.

II.
This Yuletide bustle will be less;
My school choir and an autumn show,
Releasing yet another night
For shopping with the family
Or entertaining merrily,
Releasing yet another night,
My school choir sang an autumn show;
The Yuletide bustle will be less.

III.
Just when the season's simplified,
A grandson comes to live with me,
One curious, crawling eight-month-old.
(Did Mary want to rail and rant
When Jesus dumped her favorite plant?)
One curious, crawling eight-month-old,
A grandson comes to live with me
Just when the season's simplified!

Patricia A. Laster   2003

Blackbirds of Summer

I. daybreak—
the blackbirds gossiping
just above my tent

II. the ping of sleet
on shed's tin roof—
blackbirds eating berries

III. early morning trip—
sharing the road with the blackbirds
and their breakfast

IV. a blackbird dancing
before my oncoming car

V. slower up the hill—
a blackbird in the pine

VI. early summer day—
a blackbird's shadow
walking beside me

Ruth Brooks LeCroy   1967

Leaf Fires of Autumn

Like Cherokees smoking their peace pipes,
Leaf fires of autumn are pluming the valley;
Their smoke curls and swirls and puffs out of breath,
As dragon-eyed sparks fall to their death.

The stars seem to walk on the rim of the sky,
As I watch the scene in the once verdant valley.
My thoughts soar to catch their celestial height,
While the glow from the leaf fires gladdens the night.

Though the rhythm of life changes slowly,
Even as the snow now creeps down to the valley,
And hope, like leaf ashes, lies buried for years,
There comes a tomorrow when new life appears.

Now leaves are falling and I'm yearning
For those magical scenes in the valley,
When ghostly Cherokees smoke their peace pipes,
While leaf fires of autumn are burning.

Julie Cramer Lester   1992

And Truckers Don't Cry

I couldn't help but overhear.
I was on hold,
he was on the phone next to me,
calling home.

He said,
"I called you last night, honey,
and called the night before.
There wasn't any answer.
Why aren't you ever home like before?"

"I love you, honey.
Don't you love me anymore?"

I hear the pain and puzzle
in his voice.
I wished I were someplace else.
I felt his pain as he asked,
"Honey, don't you love me anymore?"

He laid his head against the phone
and I heard him softly say,
"Kiss the kids for me, sweetheart,
tell them I'll come by someday,
and I'm sorry
you don't love me anymore."

Nancy Jane Locke   1981

Poem for an Unspoken Love

It seems you must be my lover
even though you never touch me.
I've noticed everything about you and thought,
awake and sleeping, only of you.

In the goat's milk you gave me, I tasted
your sweetness and still
have the taste of it all
inside my mouth and soul.
Do you see how easily
you give me pleasure—
and how long it lasts?

It doesn't matter if you know
nothing of this. The feeling of love is good, itself,
and makes me happy in this world.
I go on loving, independently of you.

Your thoughts enter me like
forms of clouds,
like cleansing winds,
until I am nothing inside
but a place for your presence.
Your purity is like a clean fire
in my chest. In all the cavities
of my body, you burn cleanly.

Rosa Zagnoni Marioni   1949-50

    Marooned

The trail to the gray shack is a snow slide.
Joe's truck is a white mound.
The chickens have ceased cackling.
All is silent
But for all the squeak of the rusted pulley
Where the bucket swings in the wind
Above the frozen shallow well.

In the gray shack, eyes dancing,
Children crowd at the fern-frosted window,
Looking through the moist ring
Made by their warm breaths
At the beagle hound leaping
Home through the snow,
A rabbit in his mouth.

Rosa Zagnoni Marinoni   1954-55

Timberline

Not in a grove, nor as lonesome as a pine
Rising beside a stream through mellow earth,
Not in a park, but on the timberline
Of man and beast divide, I came to birth.
The Alps, God's barrier raising to the skies,
White in the moonlight, purple in the sun,
The wind dominion where the eagle flies,
Rose to my right beyond oblivion.
Through a brown ledge of rock, my roots embrace
The hidden strata of the soul's desire,
Through which vibrates the splendor of God's face
And yellow serpentines of searing fire.
A precipice cuts through the Alps and ledge,
On which my twisted trunk leans to the gale—
Unfathomed is its depth. Between the wedge
A river rushes on through rock and shale.
Lashed by the howling winds of the divide,
The waters clear the shoals with hiss and scream...
Upon their squirming backs undaunted ride
The white feluccas of a child's own dream.

The tree strains to the wind, for well it knows
Its falling will release the melting snows.

Rosa Zagnoni Marinoni   1963

Humble Offering

The Priest is gone—
and so are the altar boys,
the crowd, the sexton,
and the beggars at the door.
The heat has been turned off.
The candles snuffed.
The doors closed.
The pews are empty
as are the choir loft,
sacristy and vestibules.
The church is empty
but for Christ.
The north wind howls,
shaking the ill-fitting windows.
The flowers on the altar cringe.
A veil of ice forms
in the Holy water bowl.

A spider drops
to the left arm-tip of the cross
and methodically starts weaving
its silver net
across the naked breast
of Christ.

Patricia Washington McGraw   1977

Me and My Shadow

I have granted myself
An honorable discharge
From humanity, for a
Brief while, that is,
So that I might take
Some time out to find
Out who/or what I am
Or wish to become.

Because I am fastidious
In my choice of companions,
I have taken the liberty
To select as my best
Friend and sole adviser,
Me, which is in itself
A kind of freedom, and
My shadow knows.

Sister Mary Ricarda McGuire, RSM   1979

Innkeeper's Dilemma

There's always one in every crowd,
and now I see
one in the motley crowd just come
from Galilee.
Men I can bed down on the floor
with little care
beyond the wine and bread and space
they take and share—
But women! They expect a place
where they can hide—
a key to lock the door against
the world outside.
And this one has a greater need.
She's numb with fright.
Herself a child, she will bring forth
a child tonight.

"I have no room for you—move on,
just go away!
No! Wait! Come back. I have a barn
and manger hay."

Sister Mary Ricarda McGuire, RSM　　　　　　　　1980

Tomorrow's Tomorrow

Good morning, Morning, eons hence;
   locked in an embryo of doubt.
      You'll come to term and be brought forth
     when years run out.

In some uncalculated pause,
   you'll move down labyrinthian ways,
      clothed in the robes of space and time—
    to greet your days.

I hope your dawning will be bright,
   unsmogged by chaos that we wrought;
     absolved from malice we allowed—
    and then forgot.

      ***

    A pulsing of life
through the dry stalks renewing
   a promise of spring.

B.J. McIntosh   1997

My Broken Heart

You strummed your guitar and sang
beautiful songs just for me
as I gazed out to purple mountains
from your desert home in February.
That was seven months ago.
Our cameras captured pictures found in nature
as you toured your mom to see horses, cattle,
fields planted proudly by you.
You introduced your neighbor, Debbie—
and I saw her eyes
lovingly follow you.
For 20 years you made molds
to pour your fantastic art—
bronze figures of your creation.
My house proudly exhibits the Indian head,
the horse, monk, wizard, the man in the tree.
I wear the long-horn cow-skull brooch.
You lived the free life
envied by the rest of us
stuck in our own captive life styles.
But does freedom mean choice
to place a gun to your head—
and to shatter my heart
and break my life, forever?

Catherine Moran   2004

Me and the Minotaur

When autumn trees bow at dusk
forming caves over the streets,
I always walk alone
discarding the day like pieces of armor
no longer needed and grown too heavy
with use.

Clothed in naked thoughts
with hair slicked back,
breasts tight against the wind,
I slice the night air with hands and feet.

It is the demon time
when I loose my ancient fears from chains,
and wrestle them once more in my mind.

It is the dark labyrinth time
when doubts become half-truths that
I must face in single combat.

With every step I chase away the monsters
of my own making
until they leave me free once more.
I pull sweaty skin tight
to contain the struggle within,
cover all scars carefully,

and follow the string home.

Catherine Moran   2005

Constructing the Building

Workmen sweat in the sun's throat and drive
cranes that reach yellowed hands into
the Earth's dirty pockets.
Dust swirls and settles on t-shirted skin.
The men haul girders and stand them in rows
like straight bones waiting for walls to cover
steel nakedness.
The sheet-rock is propped upright.
all spaces are closed in tightly.
Sunburned hands glue bricks one by one
with careless perfection along outer walls.
I watch wrists curve and slash
the mortar,
trimming excess without thinking.

Constant sun breathes down on trucks.
Concrete is guided into prearranged forms.
Then men bend their backs over gray slush,
crushing pebbles of proud cement
into walkways.
All day long they work the surface,
smoothing and smoothing until it sets firm.

One sultry day all loose ends are tied up,
and a dumpster is filled with trash.
The workmen move on without leaving a syllable.
We walk in gray suits through the glass doors,
find our desk with computers,
and complain about the dust and coffee.

Robert Moore   1976

Loneliness

To be truly alone is profound:
like the man in the news story, say,
who leans back, about to light a cigar,
when the plane's rear door is blown off
and he is sucked into space
sitting there strapped to his chair,
silent,
absurdly alive,
alone.
He watches the plane's lights fade away
and tries to decide if it is worth undoing the seat belt
or praying.

It is like that when my children leave
after their weekend with me.
the silence they leave behind
crawls across me like darkness
filtering the last light
in a dying man's eyes.

Or like at the moment of my lover's last goodbye
when I am left caressing the wind
and want to go howling and weeping to my knees
yet stand calmly on the curb fighting terror
as if I were the only fool left
and the world depended on my show of strength.

And then there is the last true loneliness
of my body wrapped in sheets
trembling on the verge of nothing,

the air dark with howls and weeping.
The pause is delicate
before the leap.

Robert Moore   1977

The Gunfighter

A gunfighter is barely hidden in my artful shadow.
As I bend owlishly over a new poem, he hunches
     crosslegged
over the heavy smell of brass casings and mounds of
     powder.
His fingers as supple as a new wound, he carefully mixes
various colored powders into the cupping brass like a poet
loving his words into weapons. As he softly fits the
     tight lead head
he lines bullets row upon row in front of his anxious gun
and stares at the poem on my page, his knuckles
     popping like shots

in the sullen room. As I revise a new poem he fingers
     his gun
gently under a bright light and begins to break it down,
brushing each piece with a fine horsehair brush and
     spreading
a thin film of oil over the tender metal until it gives
     whispers

of light into his still eyes. When the gun is put together
he weighs it solidly in his careful hand, closing his eyes
as he sights with his fingertips along the cylinder, his
     breath
shining as it smokes the polished metal. Before I go
     to a reading

he will stand for hours, first at the window, his fists
        clenching
and unclenching as he draws deep, steady breaths. Then
he will slip on tight leather gloves, tie down his holster,
and stand easily before the mirror. He will clench his fist

at his chest, drop it very slowly until it is just above
        his gun,
and then unclench it as fast as a snake's head striking.
He never touches the gun, only nods to himself, rolls
        a cigarette,
and walks out into the sunlight without a word.

As I read, he has the drop on everyone. He seldom
shoots;
only rarely, a line will set him off, he will move like a
        wolf
to someone's side, his hand will draw within a
        whisper of shaking,
and as I read, he will calmly blow them out of their chair.

Mary Hamilton Neary 1987

Ishtar Knew

All forms of life are brought with love and lust
Which wanders aimless in celestial light
Amid the morning chores or restless night,
Where dying dreams will crumble in the dust
To rise as Phoenix from the ashes' crust,
Yet helps love build a tryst with pure delight,
For Ishtar knew of love. They smile with bright
And shining eyes to watch while lovers trust
The evening pale, but finding morning sun
A picayunish sort of grace, bequeath
A clear blue dawn for lovers everywhere—
Who falsely think their love has just begun,
And will forever last. Still, underneath
Lies doubt that makes lust easier to share.

Olive Hering Nelson   1941-42

Her Man

"Put on your ruffled bonnet, Vina Jane,
And let us walk beneath the canopy of springtime,
Down the lane,"
Called Henry, as he looked in through the kitchen door.
"The bread is in the oven and I must not go too far,"
Said Vina as she took the baby from the floor.

"I want to see the fields, my dear,
And check the rows of maize,
I think the eighty will be clear,
By March we'll plant the grain,
And there will be a bumper crop
If there is rain."

So Henry broke a blossom from the low catalpa tree
And reasoned as he touched the baby's face,
Who cooed in baby glee,
"The grape vines need the tendrils cut,
The peach trees must be spayed,
The apple buds are tightly shut,
But spring is here."

So Vina tripped beside him
As they turned back up the lane
And through the trees in springtime garb
That stretched like long arms overhead,
There came the unmistaken scent
Of freshly burning bread.

Olive Hering Nelson   1941-42

Duck and Drake

Wild ducks are flying
Lost in the rain-swept night.
Their deep-toned calls re-echo
Above the city light.

Lovers watch from a window,
As a lone drake flies by
Calling his mate in the darkness,
Lost in the blue-black sky.

A drunken man goes stumbling
Avoiding the snare of police.
Around a shadowed corner
Comes a woman on caprice.

The lone duck is calling
From a mountain crest near by.
She fears the glare of the city;
The drake hears her plaintive cry.

Lovers, go back to your loving,
Woman go back to your lair,
The drake and duck are now flying
High in the open air.

Olive Hering Nelson   1963

A Sonnet to My Father's Hands

The flow of years has etched upon your hands
A pattern like the lines of reddened rust
Which threads through ageless stone but comes to dust—
Deep lines of life, like winds in prairie sands.
You once knew youth and followed its commands,
In you, who thrilled the west, a nation placed it trust.
You found out there a glory like moon-dust
That covers all the prairie and expands
Into the wind. You pushed the plow through the rain
And cut your castle from the maiden grass.
You brought a dark-eyed bride to make a home;
You knew the feel of full-brown harvest grain
Within your restless hands. You loved your lass
And built free land beneath a high blue dome.

Violette Newton   1997

Some Nights She Dreams

Some nights in the tall house
in the high Southern dark
she dreams of fire
and runs screaming
to the stairwell,
gown flying,

stops at the spindled banister
so he catches her, holds her,
turns her about and walks her back
to bed where she falls sobbing,
then sobs in his arms

while he lies there thinking
how fire started downstairs and was
not a big fire but a fire under them,
trapping them in smoke and fumes,
a fire that was out soon
for the house but not for her

and on mornings after she dreams
she goes about in silence
nose sniffing the burned smell
and shudders, wondering
what will happen on some night
when he is not there.

Hien Duc Nguyen   1979

For Your Birthday

Tomorrow will be your anniversary
day of roses
day of wines
and of interminable concerts

I am too poor: no money to buy gifts
and too illiterate: no letter I can write
but I have to share
your important day
by offering
by sending
something
something of
my little sweet dream

You have to wait for the postman
who will come
in the early morning
or in the late afternoon—whoever knows—
He should be a blue bird
or a yellow dragonfly
and you will receive
on his messenger wings
one half
the first half
of my dream
sparkling with fireworks
and stretching like clouds

You will enjoy it
lightly
softly
purely

and for the second half
of my dream
I hide it for myself

Don't ask me why
and of what it is it filled...

Opal Jane O'Neal   1980

The Transition

Is this really my father,
this tired sick old man with two days
of gray stubble on his shrunken face?

How handsome he had been:
hair, black as crow's wings,
unruly on his wide intelligent forehead;
eyes, gray as ironwood,
flecked with gold and laughter.
Each crisis had been a challenge,
each challenge an adventure.
Proud and calm he strode across the years.

Love, strong as youthful sinew,
binds me to the past, the present.

I sit in tense readiness and wait his call:
pain and fear and darkness taunt him.
He will not hear the words I speak
for age has locked him in its cell of silence,
but he will understand the touch of my hand.
I smooth his straggly hair, stroke his withered brow
and feel swelling strong within me
a strange new love.

I cradle his gnarled old hand in mine
and hum a lullaby.

Marguerite B. Palmer   1958-59

Of Polyps and Men

The coral-building polyp,
Unknowing, in his strife
Forms islands that years later
Swarm with higher life.

But men, unlike the polyp,
Are offered, as they grow,
Divinely proffered wisdom
And are equipped to know

A candle is not wasted,
Although its flame be small,
That pushes back the darkness
For anyone at all.

Marguerite B. Palmer   1961

Hoard

I know that I shall never walk this way
Again, and so I want to memorize
Each prone-to shatter, crystal winter day,
The perishable gold of springtime skies
In wake of sudden thunderstorms; the thrust
Of yellow dandelions through emerald grass,
And topaz on the trunks of pines; I must
Remember jeweled pathways as I pass.

No longer shall I squander; I shall store
A miser's hoard ear-marked indelibly;
Five hundred saffron leaves, or maybe more—
Such gold eludes definitive degree;
But with its memory, I need not fear
Bankruptcy in some future, leaner year.

Marguerite B. Palmer   1962

The Blind Song-Weaver

He did not doubt the stars
Because his eyes were blind
Nor question humankind
Because he carried scars.

A faith-engendered spark
Of radiance lit his night,
So those of us with sight
Walked bolder in the dark.

And now that he is gone,
The songs he left us suffice
To keep us thinking twice
About the dark and dawn.

Akers Pence-Moore   1986

   Toro Nagashi: August 6, 1984, Hiroshima

I walked in heart-speech silence of converging crowds
through an August darkness lit with fire-fly lanterns,
fragile as paper kites,
thin crossed strips of wood
held by a single nail that spiked a candle!
Frail tissue paper shades formed gossamer rainbow
guards
against the dark.

Along the traditional passageway
old men, bent women, clear-faced youths—
quickly, with magician-skill—
made these bright memorials to their dead
That all might share their rites,
the young, bent-old, and those with clear memory of 1945.

A growing mass, we moved,
orchestrated by a strange consent,
over Peace bridge spanning Motoyasu River
and through Peace Memorial Park.
As drops of water merge to make a moving stream,
our slow procession swelled with celebrants.
Thousands came from far-spaced cities of the earth
and formed a silent dirge by bearing gentle torches.

Recrossing Motoyasu by a second bridge,
we reached the place of entry to the water,
the forty-foot long Stairs of Stone
that line the river bank.
Quietly and careful of our wavering flames,
we formed a flow of lantern bearers
down the steep and narrow steps
to set afloat our Lights of Peaceful Rest.

To steady me, a tall New Zealander hugged my waist
as I bent to place my craft upon the current;
a tiny Indian woman touched me, to rest a moment,
as she passed me climbing up;
hands reached out to hands.

In silence I retraced the route alone,
paused on Motoyasu Bridge to watch upstream
the myriad lights massed by current into islands,
flowing tenuously slow,
twinned by reflection, magic hues upon black water,
softly bright as prism rays, primordial fire.

In the threat of Nuclear Night
Toro Nagashi lanterns glow a burning hope.

Gloria Okes Pekins   1984

Moon Rock on Display

Distant touch
of clouded, fading moon,
these moon rocks
stolen into now
out of ancient tomb.

As from Egypt's crypt
they come across the ages,
stark bone-rock
dusted, hooded
by dark queries:

Life was or never was?
Had it once begun,
how was its ending?

Moon rocks
like shards from long-dead kingdoms
smothered by eons
or powers unnamed,
a weight beyond our knowing.

Silvered relic,
moon rock
shines in the museum,
reflects our light of wonder.

We have touched the tomb.
Or the cradle.

Lily Peter   1962

For John Donne

The young schoolman dipped his pen in quicksilver
when he sat down to write of love—the young lawyer
the brilliant advocate from the Inns of Court,
self-contained, not dissolute,
burnished in Elizabethan satin,
with ruffles of fine English lawn at neck and wristband,
a great visitor of ladies,
who in turn were chided, praised, cursed, or canonized.

With the twin compasses of intellect and wit,
the slide rule of the heart's deep feeling,
the master of the trivium and quadrivium
charts the differential calculus of love,
the axis of love traced in the reticulate symbols,
in the taut concept of the twisted eyebeam
of hand-clasped lovers on a violent bank.

Seal up the moonlight in a flask, if you will,
and examine it at your leisure. The young lawyer
is not content with passion's mathematics.
He treats of love's alembic, its subtle alchemy,
the luminous shadows of its lucent spectrum,
the ionized glow that comes from the sun's center,
giving love form and substance and outward motion.

Unknown to dull sublunary lovers is this valediction
of tenderness and faith the schoolman gives us:
the naked thinking heart that makes no show;
Love inter-assured of the mind,
careless of missing eyes and lips and hands,
perfectly writing upon the air the heart's meaning.

Lily Peter   1956-57

For the Flyleaf of Emily Dickinson's Poems

Here are poems convolute as a summer shell,
Scarlet as pimpernel
Growing on a rocky ledge
At the cliff's edge—
A summer shell, that, being held to the ear,
Will make the listener hear
The murmuring of the wintry sea
Of eternity.

Lily Peter   1968

Runes for Mathematics

I: Theorem

What intricate strange flowering of the mind
is this, that, having no root thrust in the sod,
no protoplasmic gene of its own kind,
yet marvelously, as it were Aaron's rod
transfixed with almond buds and blossoms twined
in the Red Sea desert, from the mortal clod
is rapt, a frail raceme of abstract thought.
By its own germinal essence pollinated,
it becomes both the Seeker and the Sought;
the bough by which may be perpetuated
such knowledge as our random reach has brought
to living terms whereby are correlated
values and valences, with their subtle passion
for shaping matter and energy to their fashion.

II: The Second Law of Thermodynamics

My Sweet One, my Dear One, the Second Law
of Thermodynamics will have us down at last.
Make no mistake about this: the unyielding claw
of matter and energy knows its purpose; is cast
upon all-breathing and non-breathing; the raw
and corroding process that will still the fast
gold hail of our heart-beats to rust and dust and doom
but matter, it may be, is only a tatter, the worn
vestment of anti-matter, from the Ghost whose room
is Space, whose diadem is Time, the dimension torn
from the fabric of being, from whence comes all the bloom

and beauty of the universe, present and future, borne
from the penumbra of mystery shrouding the Ghost,
matter, energy, our love, that is more and most!

III: RE: Numbers

Never trust numbers: they are inclined to nil,
and what they communicate is not all-divining.
Weigh up the flower—its sheen is missing still,
Count all the quantums when the sun is shining—
you will not find the image of the wooded hill
reflected in the lake, the peony lining
of the cumulus cloud crowning the hilltop height.
Numbers have their own mystique: each integer,
beginning with zero, goes of its will bedight
as the sum of four squares, the sum of nine cubes.
Infer if you will, why, and look for the learned light
to show why nineteen fourth powers choose to concur
in every whole number from one to the last decillion,
but there is no number for joy in any million!

Alice Waddell Portis   1954-55

Farmhouse Ghosts

Of nothing, now, the grey, old farmhouse boasts
But the emptiness and solitude and ghosts,
Ghosts of promises that came with springs,
Of blighted faith in heavy harvestings,
Ghosts, where now the echoes sell the gloom,
And ride the emptiness from room to room.

Through the snaggle-toothed old fence they come,
      sneaking,
Up the weathered walls they climb, creaking,
Around the door posts fleshless arms are wrapping,
Up against the window panes their fingers tapping.

But never show the Negro boys these "ha'nts",
For they will come in June in ragged pants
With 'lasses pails of clean and shiny tin;
They'll never mind the briers that tear their skin
Like wicked, phantom claws. Oh! Never tell!
For they see only berries there—to sell.

Alice Waddell Portis　　　　　　　　　　　　　　1956-57

Hunter in the Valley

Over my head the giant mountain looms,
Deriding me for such a timid quest—
Hunting helpless quail with dog and gun.
"Such childish sport!" He scoffs; he bares his chest
And shows whole forests growing there
And granite muscled ribs. Loudly he cries,
"Try chasing storm clouds down the vale, or gulping
Lightning bolts like toad frogs swallow flies,
Or zipping up a mile-deep pocket fast
With ninety smothering miners still inside.

So sport is what you like? Try shouldering
The sun by day, the moon at eventide,
Dispatch an avalanche or play the game
Of echo with a million wildlife calls.
Try teaming up with tumbling clouds to sire
A river and a dozen waterfalls."

Over my head the mighty mountain towers
Whose majesty and strength I cannot scale;
I lift my eyes unto the God-made hills
And walk more humbly down the valley trail.

Gladys Powell   1954-55

Seacoast Honeymoon

All through the night we heard the splash and roar,
A wild sea monster, chained to ocean bed,
Hurled waves of envy on our cabin door
In anger, centuries old, moon madness fed.
Then, turning with the tide, a lash of tail
Beat surf house high. This din and deviltry
Made panic-prayers last through the whirling gale,
Stealing our happiness, like shivaree.

When morning came, the demon storm had died;
The sun brought back assurance to the land.
Again the gulls outlined the blue and cried.
Both laughing, we ran barefoot down the sand,
Gathering cast-up shells for souvenirs;
Our love made stronger for our night of fears.

Gladys Powell   1956-57

Language of Light

All growing plants with roots held fast in slime,
Whose arms reach patiently toward the sun,
Unfold their flowers, bud to bloom, in time
For morning miracles for everyone.

Our personalities will also grow
Into tranquility through interludes
Of quiet search for woods we want to know
As beautiful as the Beatitudes.

Jean Ravenscroft   1993

A Gentle Poet

Her blond, sun-streaked, dark-rooted hair
is tethered at the crown,
rubber-banded, perched off-center—
a thirty-five year face framed in
uncontrolled leftovers
like scattered chaff of wheat.

The "permanent wave" has long since given up.
It bends and S-curves down in haphazard abandon
while scraggly swatches catch
in the button at her neck.

She walks as if to thrust each foot
into an imaginary hole,
a laborious toeing-in gait,
in grey tie-flats with worn crepe soles.

In her pudgy nail-bitten hand is clutched
a chocolate bar wrapped in blue and white,
a brightness to further dull
the drab dress of doubtful ownership
and sweater whose buttons drag one side
to form an arrow to the shoes.

She climbs the three worn steps
as if to board a wagon bound for town.
Her chocolate bar aside,
she presses rumpled papers to the podium
as pale blue eyes with sagging lids
scan for sympathetic signs.

She speaks.
And though her outer looks deny,
her voice affirms: "I dream, I love, I am,"
and the room becomes her hushed arena.

Bonnie Reynolds   1987

    In Defense of You

I do not mind you—
small yellow blossom.
  In your quiet,
    unobtrusive way you bring my day
      to bloom, array my yard
      and hue my life.

When you arrive, I become alive.
I know your gold will turn my cold heart warm
And I will burn renewed.

        I will be intoxicated
        with living
        like drunken bees
        swaggering to hives
      from racy
      dandelion wine.

I do not mind you—weed.
Feed me spring.

When your head turns white
I, like the wind,
  will spread your silver hair to air
  and make a wish.

Clovita Rice   1969

Difference

War war war
This was a word
I scarcely heard,
perhaps was vaguely
aware of on the front page
as I rummaged through the paper
to find Dennis the Menace,
the Wizard of Id,
or what's on sale where...
War is a neon word
you see like sun spots
when a son, husband, brother
is drawn toward
its heated circumference...
and the heart closets itself
repeatedly to pray
that wings not made of wax
will shield them
from the fire.

Marnelle Haynes Robertson								1972

Earth-Hunger

I bring the woods home, cupped within my hand:
a bit of bark, a nut, mossy stone,
a lump of clay, a frond of fern, a rose
(the homely country cousin of the buds
that grace the greenhouse); yet the spell is gone.
The sudden whir of wings among the brush
I cannot bring, nor driftwood on the shore
(except a sample out of context), nor
lake water lapping lazily on the bank,
nor tiny, scared things scurrying down to drink.
And yet when I am empty to the core,
too far away to follow the winding road
back to the source to still that primal need
for dark, damp earth beside a dripping spring,
this talisman becomes for me a shrine
and I am filled—almost—until the keen
earth-hunger comes again.

Marnelle Haynes Robertson   1993

Matilda Jekyll

I was a female bigamist.
Married properly in church
to a well-known doctor.
I had another man
whom I kept secret.
At least I tried.
My husband was a good provider.
I did not need to worry
about grocery bills or taxes.
And when he died,
he had a long obituary,
listing causes he had sponsored
and honors won.

I was the quiet wife
no one could fathom.
I stayed home, and then
when I must go,
covered my bruises
with bright makeup and a smile.
And later,
even the neighbors did not guess,
as I sat chuckling in the corner,
writing my poems, that I
was also the widow
of Mr. Hyde.

Barbara Robinette   2002

We Played Gin Rummy

for money
every spring Saturday
afternoon until three
or until you
grew too tired.

I won the set. You cheerfully
paid your eight dollars owed.
In July, we buried you.

I kept the eight dollars alone
in a box in my room
until I was forty-two and,

thinking of you, I purchased your
posthumous present.

Every morning I sip warm
coffee in your presence.

Pearl Lunt Robinson   1954-55

Uncomforted

No one saw his tears. He wept
after he closed the door:
but in a little town, they knew
he wept, and what for.

Love that stood beneath the wall
his flinty gaze erected,
always stood outside; he dealt
with grief as he elected.

Alone, he learned how thin a thread
endurance sometimes is:
weeping for one's lost Israel,
as Moses wept for his.

Immortal wings brushed Moses, sweet
comfort in their stir.
Even the wings of heaven skirted
this New Englander.

Pearl Lunt Robinson   1955-56

    Anonymous

I tell his Latin name with pride.
I do not know who lived inside
this polished shell. He left no trace...
no sign to set him from his race.
House-bound, he toured the ocean floor:

ocean above, behind, before.
Independent and aloof,
underneath this fluted roof,
he ate and slept and breathed his breath:
he lived his life and died his death.

Who was at home, a horn to blow
sea-music on, I do not know.

Constance Rollins Rouse 1961

The Promise

We followed the narrow path—
its frozen ruts
prodding our feet along;
the north wind, like a vicious dog,
snapped and bit,
as we stopped at the fresh-turned grave.
Then I heard
the giant hemlock shuddering—
tall guardian
of my sleeping generations, shuddering—
Late in the night,
snow came tossing a downy comforter
gently over the place.

The next day I went back,
my footsteps, softly cushioned now,
making a feathery track
in the glittering white.
And I heard the hemlock whispering—
whispering a promise:
"As surely as the greening spring
comes to heal an ugly earth wound,
time will help to heal a wounded heart."

Marie Morris Rushing   1947-48

Mental Celibacy

If I am not good,
If I am not kind,
Perhaps I am wood,
Maybe I am blind.

For your eyes have said
That the lips have lied,
And the thoughts heart-fed,
By glance is implied.

That the touch proclaims,
More than words desire,
With fervor that shames,
A rhetorical fire!

If I am not good,
Then I must be kind,
For stoic as wood,
I evade your mind.

Marie Morris Rushing   1949-50

Grandfather Knelt

Wounded on every side the giant oak stood
Its sap-wood broken by the biting saw
Medullary rays of mauve-tinted wood,
Strained taut against an ever-widening jaw.

John placed the wedge then swung the heavy mall
And when the single, silver-tooth of death
Severed the heartwood, facing from its fall,
Grandfather turned, exhaled a snorting breath.

Now leaning westward in the cobalt sky
The great tree shuddered, with spasmodic sound
It clutched at nothingness, its rasping sigh
Ending in thunderous oaths along the ground...

John smiled and said, "It was a stubborn tree."
Grandfather knelt, with gnarled thumb traced each ring.
His drawn face paled, "Two hundred twenty-three!"
Lifted his cap as to a fallen king.

Marie Morris Rushing   1966

Furrow of Discontent

I think my father died before his time
When supermarkets whittled the trout brook
From the east forty; agents offered lime
For remaining acreage; he got that look
Of fear, confusion, which I never knew;
Urban renewal banished fowl and cow:
"Not one gray mule is left to follow through
The springtime, not even a rusty plow."
I think he might have lingered for a spell
But city limits rolled like Moses' sea
Swallowed his land, and when the great trees fell
I think my father withered inwardly...
At my insistence he moved into town;
He vowed, "The sun does neither rise nor set;
Someone has turned the growing earth around."
And more than once his faded eyes were wet.
Wretched, restless, he watched that final spring,
Fretted in sleep of a planting thunder
Where no one plowed or sowed a single thing,
'Til discontent furrowed my father under...

Ruth Wilson Scholl									1971

    Frozen Landscape

How sad it seems,
This frozen landscape on my easel here.
It does not speak to me.

I feel no turbulence of winds,
No air through which doves might wheel
Or rains could sluice
And gentle snows could sift
And whirl in blizzards' disarray
Or sun's bright shafts could spear the land
With sharp relief of roving shapes of clouds.

The ancients too were not content
With gods who smiled in perpetual peace,
Free of Jove's thunderbolts
And Diana's arrows
And winged horses plunging up and up...

So I shall try again
And let my brushes lacerate the placid scene
With vibrant light and color
Until my painting moves and laughs
And speaks to me.

Mary Bathus Schriver   1951-52

Winter Trees

They stood, tall silhouettes,
Against a cold gray sky;
No sign of life in trunk or limb
As chilling gales swept fiercely by.

Grim, powerless in the wintry wind,
They swayed in calm expectant mood—
Like listeners to orchestral strains
For well-loved theme or interlude;

Awaiting time when to their roots,
The life sap springing rich and deep,
Will ooze through veins to each small stem,
And waken buds now fast asleep;

Awaiting green leaves, royal robes
To rustle in the summer breeze
While nesting bird and insect claim
The tribute only given by trees.

And their great roots beneath the soil
Await the press of tired feet
Of man or herd, that in their shade
Will pause and seek a cool retreat.

They stood, tall silhouettes,
Against a cold gray sky.
Only their upturned branches told
The perennial hopes that in them lie.
Would that we, too, like winter trees,

Stripped of our gems by life storms, wild
Could wait, as they, with souls uplift,
Expectant, faith-sure, strong and mild.

Gladys Tillman Scott   1967

A Song to David

David, son of Jesse,
Hasten to my rescue;
I am buffeted on either side
By incompetence.
Lend me your leather-thonged sling
Loaded with diamond-edged
Pebble of understanding.
Steady my hand, O David,
As I strive to slay the dragon
Of illiteracy.
May the missile be swift and sure.
As plasma flows from the fallen foe,
May it rise again in a snowy-white mist
Forming plumes of Love, Prudence
And the mind of Human Kindness.
Then may I, in deep humility
Gather them up and lay them
At the throne of everlasting knowledge.

Dorrill Scroggin   1939-40

Psyche

I come to you
Out of the twilight
With the last pale ray of the sun;
I'm borne to you
On the wings of Dusk,
And you feel me
In the lengthening shadows,
In the cool
Breath of earth.

I am a glance
In eyes you cannot forget;
I am a fragrance
Which even yet pervades
The air you breathe;
I am a bit
Of deep, clear laughter;
I am a moment
Of lashing despair;
I am a cherished instant
Of supreme ecstasy;
I am borne to you,
Down the years,
On the wings of Dusk.

Diana Sherwood   1944-45

Music

The soft night rain has changed to sleet
And tinkles on the window glass
Like castanets in fairy hands;
I am loath to have its magic pass.

Home sounds blend into harmony;
The clock, the fire, the children's play;
Faint dripping from the eaves make time
And rhythm in this roundelay.

Outside, the pines swish in the wind.
Through mist, a far bell sends its call.
The motor murmurs in the drive,
Dear voices greet us from the hall.

    The sounds that we have loved for years
    Become sweet music to the ears.

Richard Leon Spain   1949-50

Night Journey

As we rode the lean white highway through the dark
Hearing the motor-song, the heavy whisper of tires
On concrete, and were lulled and put at peace
Beneath the benevolent brooding stream of telephone
      wires,
Suddenly we saw at the stony margin of the road
A moving flash as of thousands of turquoise fires.
These were the eye of spiders marching evenly—
A fragile tide advancing on brittle feet,
Huddled for courage, unhaltingly paced to meet
The fury of the night with equal wrath.
And yet another headlight, hours from now,
Will catch their glow but little farther down the path.

Unthinking and savage race, aware of man,
Stirred by the norther of his headlong flight,
Stung by the quick dust from his flying wheels;
Rejectful of his schemes yet giving dumb salute
As they turn unflinching jeweled eyes to his light—
A proud and bitter caravan they press together
Making their way beside his road of stone,
Far-flung across their maples green abodes,
Serving as dark a purpose of their own.

Thomas Sperling   1946-47

November Dirge

The wind is shaking from weary branches
The ashes of autumn, shriveled and dry;
The green has faded from field and meadow—
This is the season when all things die.

Denuded tree-limbs, gaunt and shivering,
Rattle like wings of a skeleton bird;
Bleak is the landscape; bleak is my spirit,
Bitter my thoughts beyond power of word.

There is an ache that comes with November,
Keen with the voices of green things dying,
Shrill as the cry of wild fowl departing,
Dead as withered leaves everywhere lying.

The heart in kinship with outdoor creatures,
The heart in tune with the wood-voices call
Shares every pang as they pale and perish,
Droops low and falls as the shrunken leaves fall.

Helene Stallcup 1985

The Power Switch

When winter cracks its cannon on the air
The soft earth shivers in a frightened chill
And basely cedes all men to winter's will
By lowering it colors everywhere.
The new regime is drastic if you dare
Be caught outside your private domicile
Clad in light uniforms of summer, still.
A cat-o-nine tails wind awaits you there.
But conquered men who prudently succumb
To chill authority escape the blow
Of winter's ills, and find it offers some
Appeasements like warm fires and feathered snow
    With one gold though to pass the tedium,
    If winter comes, then it must surely go.

Helene Stallcup   1991

Fish Eggs in Oil

The words of men are like fish eggs in oil,
as hard to catch, impossible to hold.
They may be beautiful and fine as foil,
the solid truth, and spendable as gold,
but one cannot be pinned upon the plate
nor fastened to the table with a tape.
Both pauper and the president may state
their tales with ample margin to escape,
for promises will not sit on the shelf,
stay edible for half a dozen years.
The truth is faithful servant to the self,
and with advantage often disappears,
    for rather than stand up and give offense,
    it slips beneath the oil of verb and tense.

Harding Stedler   2002

Equatorial Silence

I people watch
outside the coffee shop
as folks move aimlessly
among peach petals
that waft confetti-like
where spring explodes.
Tourists pass
without a nod,
in silence,
strangers in a land
of earthy bean smell
and exotic candle scents.
They travel at varied gaits
in shoes
sewn by Mexican women
for sacks of tortilla flour.
They bounce too many pounds
on waistlines needing pruned
and reconfigured.

This equator turns its back
on breathing suns,
eager to lure old men
from under palm trees
to gather singing seashells
beside the dark
where even sand is still.

Harding Stedler   1999

Nightmare Precluding Dreams

Shiver me gray, November,
with Canadian gusts
driving southbound geese
across the Plains.
Parchment clings in desperation
to once-supple branches.
I wake at night
to mischief in the trees,
whose leaves resist your swirls.

I cannot sleep
for turmoil in the dark.
Even the mournful sounds
of freight trains
are swallowed by the wind.

You paint for me a nightmare
that precludes
the innocence of my dreams.
I walk the floor,
stare through window-darkness,
and reach for creaking limbs
of sycamore.

Kathryn S. Stone   1955-56

Fulfillment

I walked a path in the gentle wind
And found it jeweled by the rain.
A bob-o-link in the budding boughs
Warbled a wistful new refrain.

While I walked slowly down the way
I felt the fingers of the air.
Perhaps in hiding was a fay
Guarding a precious treasure there?

And then I found a wakened spring
Flowing cool waters sparkling clean.
Around its edge were bits of heaven
A votive planted for its queen.

Johnye E. Strickland   1992

Mother and Child

Startled by the stillness in the house,
the mother turned toward the window, searched
the yard. Failing to find the missing child,
she stuck her needle in the half hemmed blouse,
rose, and started to the door to scan the street.
The child in the next room saw her mother move
and slipped into the closet to surprise her.
She heard the footsteps cross the polished floor,
the latch lifted, the screen, pushed open, screak.
She heard her name called in anger, then in dread.
She nudged the closet door open a crack,
looked out, and saw her mother's silhouette
mater doloroso of the West.

Johnye E. Strickland   1996

Recurring Dream

As a child I repeatedly dreamt
about my own death.
The dream always began
with me running as hard as I could
around a low lying mountain,
chased by a herd of red cows.

Some nights this was all I saw,
but I could hear their hooves
pounding the yellow-brown calechi,
matching the rhythm of the pumps
in the neighboring oil field.

Eventually they began to gain on me
until one night they caught up,
the point runner butting me up
toward Heaven, her horn
tearing a hole in the skirt
of my new plaid dress.

Heaven was a square wooden structure
with a porch across the front
like the open tailgate on a pickup.
Newcomers had to lie on this porch
covered with blue blankets
until they had been properly processed.
Some of the other waiting children
told me I wouldn't be allowed to enter
because I hadn't been vaccinated.

Lew Taylor   2003

False Stones

Riding the rails for three long years
Has made a hobo lean,
But he's learned the code of the open road
And what the clan signs mean.

Today he tramps a railroad town
Hoping to cadge his lunch.
He's tired of the brew and mulligan stew
He shares with the jungle bunch.

He looks for signs that mark a house,
Signs brethren have placed before,
Where a lady cooks and trusts the looks
Of a hard-luck troubadour.

He sees four stones laid on a line:
"This house is a friendly place."
With a tale to tell he rings the bell
Then quietly states his case.

She hears in silence his earnest plea,
Will provide him with a meal. But
Out in the back by the garden shack
Is a stack of wood he must first cut.

He sees the saw and peers at the pile
Considering what to say;
Then shivers his bones, scatters the stones,
And sadly walks away.

Diane Taylor   1980

The Calling

I know an autumn mountain
Safely veiled in calico
With a wild and shining river
For a ribbon curled below.

At dusk a she-wolf pauses
To sip the frosty air,
As, misty eyed, the mountain
Lets down her auburn hair.

A shadow fox on silent paws,
His eyes like amber flint,
Comes ghosting to the creek to taste
Cold water, spiced with mint.

Come with me to my mountain
When the pain's too much to bear
And sorrow sears your spirit—
Close your eyes and meet me there.

Dell Teeter   1949-50

When April Knocks

When April knocks upon my door,
I swing it open wide,
And cast my worries out to sea,
To drift on with the tide.

I go in search of simple things,
A bud, a nesting bird—
To see a seed push through the earth
Where mellow ground was stirred.

I like to watch the world awake,
And dawn fold night away,
And see a cloud tinged with the sun
Turn to a perfect day.

The simple things of life are best;
One need not travel far,
To see the moon through cypress trees,
A sunset or a star.

Valeria Browne Thornton   1971

    RFK

Though rich, he felt the hunger of the poor;
Could see with the eyes of migrant worker crews;
Could taste the squalor ghetto tots endure;
Could walk the barren soil in red men's shoes.
Though loved, his tender heart could empathize
With those unlovable, could recognize
The bitter verities that made them hate.
Though strong, he knew the terrors of the weak;
Their toughly forthright advocate and friend,
He fought in their behalf for power's peak—
Yet some folks called him "ruthless" to the end.
    He needs no monument. We'll see him stand...
    Worn face, and rumpled hair, and outstretched
        hand.

Valeria Browne Thornton   1982

To Peter I. Tchaikovsky

I heard my best-loved symphony again—
Your Fifth, in all its violence and grace—
With wonder at your timeless power to brace
A spirit grappling with misfortune's pain.
Once more, I lived a night of dismal rain,
Humiliated, crushed, afraid to face
The years in which I seemed to have no place,
Till music captured misery's domain.
Out of a lonely and ill-fated life
There sprang the splendor of your masterpiece,
Harmonic sword to hold despair at bay.
As you met woes with orchestrated strife,
My sonnets and my ballads must not cease
To feed those flames of hope in their small way.

Valeria Browne Thornton   1992

    Misplaced Woman

How can a woman live without some place
to make a home, for this has been her flair
since Eve, cast out of Eden in disgrace,
encountered cold, and danger, and despair.
A woman needs a door that she can lock,
a little kitchen, and some friendly light;
is lost without a calendar and clock,
a pillow, pleasant music, peaceful night.
She has an instinct to express herself
without obstruction, and to decorate;
requires a hoard-away or showing shelf
as treasures of the heart accumulate.
    A foot loose man may bed down in a box,
    but homeless woman is a paradox.

Ninagene Tillery   1983

   All That Remained Were Reminders of Death

I climbed the fence when I ran
out of road, found the house,
paneless, stuffed with hay. The mud chimney
lay in lumps, half hidden
by cow-chips and clumps of cattle stamped
weeds. I tried to see inside
where once a rough blue table with bench
across the back took up half
the kitchen. I tried not
to hear sounds she made that day.
Some things need to be stored.

I leaned against the porch post, called back
bits, pieces of my family caught
on bleached boards, empty hinges:
my father (dark with Indian-black hair, hazel eyes)
bent, straightened near
a bed where some strange woman
wore my mother's face.
I saw two girls
with tight French braids being shuffled
off to town by frozen-faced neighbors
who offered pink
paper parasols, chocolate ice cream
in exchange for the tastes and sounds of death.

Ninagene Tillery   1996

Married Misfits

"Six weeks, tops," they wagered.
"Different as left and right."
Ignoring predictions of gloom
and doom, we danced like fireflies,
stung like bees. Slammed receivers,
called right back. Held each other
until anger was laughter, wool became
satin, icicles were steam.

The road ahead curved like a cashew,
the horizon was a lady's orchid scarf.
Time tumbled quickly as winter rock
slides, bets were called, wagers paid.

Lying together in the darkness,
comfortable as freshly laundered socks,
remembering gritty sleeping bags and
cacti...old lovers shake with
laughter and the same shooting stars.

Anita E. Turner					1946-47

Enchantment

You played upon my heart
As on the strings of a golden lyre;
It was like a mid-summer night's dream.
You brought forth melodies deep,
Enchanting, soft and sweet
As the symphonies of another world.
So was my love for you.

You broke those strings,
And did not turn to mend.
Perhaps you played as deftly on another heart;
We understand.

You came to me in reverie
And asked to take those strings again
And play the melodies that might have been;
Like the soft whispering pines under
The spell of a lover-sharing moon;
But alas! An abyss—
My love was gone for you.

Patsy McKenzie Turner   1985

Common Factors

When I was a curious student
And heard that saucy number
That divides into a greater number,
Divides and divides,
So that three-fifteenths
Is really one-fifth
And two-fourths
Is really one-half.
I thought it strange
Because in my youth
I had not known grief
Or humility or loss;
I didn't know the human divisors
Common to all our parts
Scattered across the earth.
I later learned that reduction
Is the best way to become prime.

Neva McMillan Upton   1942-43

A Soldier's Love Letter

Tomorrow I die,
But tonight I think of you
And all the gay inconsequential things we shared
That made youth fair.

Remembering an afternoon in mid-July
When streamers of dust lay thick
In the sunlight's path,
And you, in a dress of palest green,
Tripped as we climbed the weathered gate
To the orchard lane
And fell, by chance into my arms;
Remembering the exquisite perfectness
That moment gave,
I wish you to know
That such are the thoughts a man takes
Into eternity.

Tomorrow I die;
But tonight I think of you.

Peggy Caudle Vining   1969

    Thanksgiving Time

It's harvest time again throughout the land
And muscadines are hanging on the vine.
A pumpkin moon hangs on a velvet band
Of night, and apples smell as pungent wine.
The corn is shocked and ready to be hauled
And farmers count to tally up their yield.
The hills echo the sounds that birds have called
To tell that grain is scattered in the field.
The harvest has been plentiful this year
And once again the bounty store is great;
The farmers smile at last because their fear
Is gone...no longer do they have to wait.
    The time is here at last for restful living
    And singing out the praises of Thanksgiving.

Peggy Caudle Vining   1989

Prolific Dandelions

There is enough fluff in your roundness to:
    Stuff a tobacco sack,
    Make me sneeze...
    Populate a hillside
    In a quick breeze.
    Entice me to laughter
    If I should blow,
    And forever after...

Cause you to grow!

Ida Crane Walker   1997

Rx: Antidote for Loneliness in Children

I read to them each night before they sleep
from books as varied as the minds they roam;
Walt Whitman poems stand beside BoPeep,
mysterious Poe right there to chill the bone.
Their love of books will never wane with time
because I cared enough to give myself
to lead the way through labyrinths of rhyme
and magic tunnels through the nine-foot shelf.
   The hours they spend alone will be well spent,
   never lonely if there's a book in print.

Jo Van Dalsem Wells   1950-51

Broken Lute

I chose with care the words that I would say
And I would bring them as a friendly gift,
Like myrrh and incense that might help to lift
The darkness of your night and speed the day.

Now I have knocked upon your wreath-draped door
And crossed into this flower-scented room
(With only candles to dispel the gloom)
To bring trite words that you have heard before.

If you would wonder why I do not speak;
Why, wordlessly, I only touch your hand,
I hope that somehow you will understand
I find my words—all words—are much too weak.

Now I, the word-wise one, am stricken mute
Before you—voiceless as a broken lute.

Minnilu Whitington						1948-49

Day's End

I love the ending of the day,
When all the tools are put away,
The supper over, dishes done,
To sit beside that certain one
Upon the door-step; while he thinks
I watch the sun as down it sinks,
And hear the lowing of the cows,
The peaceful grunting of the sows,
The Negroes as they home-ward plod
And sing their songs of love and God.
   I love the ending of the day—
Oh may it always be this way.

Elizabeth Wilkey						1940-41

On Hearing Wagner's *Tristan and Isolde*

What mighty power
Would raise the artist's hands
To bare, thereon, his hungry soul
And precious thoughts
To men who sneer
But hunger too?

What gossamer dream
Would brush those pallid fingers
But leave them empty still?

Perhaps that God is wise
Who knows his form
Is not a worthy prize,
And leaves amorphous passion
Taunting par-eyed beggars
Who stumble after.

JoAnne Rennells Wilson   1970

Morning on the Lake

The lake is calm in morning
Rippling at touch of my oar.
Yellow coins of aspen trees
Are scattered along the shore.

Picket rows of birches
Uniformed in white
Cast their ghostly likeness
In the water's flickering light.

The dark-eyed minnows,
Playing in schooling flocks,
Shoot like shining darts
Between glossy rocks.

High in the sea of silver,
Like a ship of pulsing souls,
The sun-glinted Mallards cry—
Sailing to charted goals.

Mamie Lou Wisener   1952-53

The Clock Has Ticked

If I could lift the latch again
To our own little cottage door,
And find you waiting there for me
Like you always did before.

I would make amends for all the past—
I know now I was wrong—
I would love to take you in my arms,
And make your life a song.

But now the clock has ticked its time,
My heart ticks sadly too—
The hours would not seem half so long,
If I could be with you.

It does not matter where you are,
How far we live apart—
You will always hold that unseen key
To my imprisoned heart.

Anna Nash Yarbrough   1960

Face to the Sunrise

I want my home upon this hill where I
May face the east. Before the morning sun
Has touched the valley bed, a golden sky
Will quicken me to duties to be done.
I want my lawn unhampered by tall shrubs
So I can see the road and pause amid
My tasks to lay aside my brooms and tubs
And tell a neighbor of a new born kid
A nanny-goat has dropped. I want a wide
Backyard to give my children space for play.
My Love, I plan this home with grateful pride,
This hill-top home to face the break of day,
And know though hours grow dark and night
      grows long
Each bright sunrise will lift our hearts to song.

Kitty Yeager   1989

Home for the Funeral

As moonlight sparkles snow on cherry trees
Like flocks of sequin fire in comet swirl,
I see you walking, slightly bowed at knees,
Through greening woods beside a little girl,
With delta soil encrusting working boots.
You stoop for violets where mosses race
And blue my tiny hands with fragrant shoots
As grand as fairy queens in purple lace!
The house you built with trim of gingerbread
Is cracking weathered wood in winter chill,
Where part of me is warm in childhood bed
And part of me is cold on Heather Hill.
    As soon as ices melt to rivulets,
    I'll come with doves to bring you violets.

Lavon Yepez   1987

Whirling Candy Stripes

My marble playground sparkled
like skater's ice for my gliding soles.
In one slide, I'd skim across the floor—
more fun than tumbling over knolls.

No honeysuckle trailed along my path,
but clouds of Mennen's talc perfumed the air,
blending with Jeris' Wild Root mist
combed through a client's hair.

Music? No background rock, no radio, no T.V.;
just rhythmic strokes of flannel stripes
popping in syncopated beat and
heavy metal sounds of scissor's snips.

Astride my mount of brass and leather
I'd spin my private carousel
faster than the whirling candy stripes
that cast me in their spell.

Between shampoos, haircuts and shaves,
Dad's fragrant hands caressed my head—
a father's touch to show his love,
no need for words he left unsaid.

Gretchen Youmans   1975

This Gold

Enlarge my sight these autumn days
To see the wonder of this gold.
Alert my senses to absorb
This mellowed wealth—and let me hold
It in extended arms—not stow
It back, but where each sunshine ray
Can touch it, and through windows clear
And joyous, send reflected glow
Into a darkened winter day,
That people groping as they go
May find a lighted way
And banish fear.
Let me return each grain unstored,
And never hoard this gold.

Poets' Roundtable of Arkansas

About the Editor

Marck L. Beggs earned his Ph.D. from the University of Denver, his M.F.A. from Warren Wilson College, and currently is a professor of English at Henderson State University. He lives by a pond in Pulaski County, Arkansas, with his wife and a number of strange animals. Beggs is the author of three collections of poetry: *Catastrophic Chords, Libido Café,* and *Godworm.* He is also a member of the folk-rock duo, Bohemian Sauce, and he was named one of the "ten sexiest vegetarians over 50" by PETA in 2009. His wife, Carly, is one hot tomato.

If you'd like to know more about Poets of the Roundtable of Arkansas visit The Encyclopedia of Arkansas History and Culture at:
www.encyclopediaofarkansas.net

CPSIA information can be obtained at www.ICGtesting.com
Printed in the USA
LVOW08*2321071013

355825LV00002B/2/P